NOBODY

WANTS TO DIE

Biographical Highlights

depicting the true story of Israel

-by-

Henry Ben-Dov

I'm not a politician or a diplomat. Not being one implies that facts, rather than lies and spin, are the subject of this narrative. The time has come to tell the story of Israel's struggles from the point of view of one who lived through it.

Copyright by Henry Ben-Dov

Second printing 2013

===

Dedicated to Lehi & Etzel underground fighters who sacrificed their lives to create and sustain the State of Israel.

===

****

Many thanks to Lehi fighter Haim Shalom Levy for being the first to hoist the Israeli flag in Jerusalem.

****

Published by NHBD Publications

THE TRUTH AND NOTHING BUT THE TRUTH

In his foreign press conference, Scientist-Professor Chaim Weitzman, the first President of Israel, was asked how, in his opinion, can the government secure the miniscule new state. Considering that the number of Israel's population, barely half a million, faced a hostile Muslim population of about 200 million, the physical survival of the infant state was in doubt.

The question was pertinent in particular that thirteen Muslim states declared war against tiny Israel. These states had modern Armies, Air-Forces and Navies with up-to-date equipment and unlimited supplies, while at that time Israel had no Army, Equipment, Trained military personnel, no Navy and no Air-Force to speak of.

As for Israel's air-power, the Israeli Air-Force consisted of four fighter planes assembled from old German Messerschmitt wrecks (used by Nazis as their main Fighter Plane) collected by Israeli mechanics from junkyards in Germany. The parts were brought to Israel, assembled, improved, and tested with the intention to use them in combat against a combined hostile Muslim force of hundreds.

Military experts predicted that Israel will last no longer than six months. Even that was considered doubtful. Looking at the numbers involved, Israel had no chance, period.

The biggest challenge was the Egyptian Air-Force. Updated by Britain with many first class Spitfire Squadrons of Fighter Planes, it was a safe bet that Israel would be devastated and defeated. What was the determining factor: a miracle or pilot skills? No one knew for sure. However, when push came to shove, and the Egyptian Air-force attacked the Israeli ground forces in the south full force, the pitiful Israeli planes decimated them all.

The author of this narrative was one of the ground forces witnessing this miraculous air battle. The professor's answer as to the future of fragile Israel left most people speechless when he stated, **"Let the future take care of the future."** His answer prompted many Israelis to doubt whether he was the most qualified individual to be president.

The president was a brilliant scientist, and the International Scientific Community agreed, but his casual remark about the future of Israel served enemies of the Jewish State well. The hostile forces concluded that with such lax leadership Zionism was vulnerable. The encouragement the professor provided was like a shot in the arm to Yassir Arafat's PLO and his followers, not to mention all other radical Islamic organizations mobilizing their forces in wait for a chance to pounce on tiny Israel. Almost David and Goliath all over again.

Professor Weitzman helped the British Empire save the lives of British soldiers during the First World War when he invented the Gas Mask for use by their armed forces. As long as he served British interests the professor was praised by the British Press as well as the authorities. Many hoped that his loyalty to the British Crown will be appreciated, perhaps even rewarded, in particular that the Nazis murdered any human with a trace of Jewish blood.

After all, how many Arab or Muslim Scientists contributed to British interests throughout history?

Not even one.

How many of them contributed to the war effort?

Not even one.

How many D'Israelis did the Arabs or Muslims provided for the benefit of the British Empire?

Not even one.

And yet, when it came to life and death of the professor's own people, did British politicians do anything to reciprocate?

Not even one!

When Hitler's Germany brutalized and cremated six million Jews in Europe, including children and babies, and it was no longer a secret that it's actually happening, the Great British Empire paid the professor back right away in a typical British way: Britain refused to allow the professor's brothers and sisters, namely refugees fleeing the Nazis, to immigrate to the Land of Israel which, for selfish political reasons, they called Palestine, not Eretz Israel (the Land of Israel) evidenced by the Bible and history confirmed by archeological digs throughout the ages.

Historical facts and eye-witness accounts confirm that Elite British forces indirectly supported the Nazis as well as Arab interests by doing their dirty work: they sunk refugee boats, beat and crippled old men, women and children in their attempt to force them to go back to where they came from.

The British Government knew that when the Nazis get them back they'll be sent to the ovens like others before them. There's no chance of denial by British sympathizers because many a time my friends and I witnessed the "humane" British treatment of refugees with our own eyes. That's the reason we joined the undergrounds against the British in proportionally big numbers.

How many British Politicians tried to help?

None whatsoever.

Not then, not even now.

In order to legalize their behavior they introduced a law called **"The White Paper"** whereas a maximum of 100,000 Jewish refugees only will be allowed into the country. Six million Jews were turned to ashes as well as soap, and many of them would have been saved if they were allowed to land, but Great Britain produced no one among their enlightened leaders to protest or even express a will to help.

Once the quota would be implemented, anyone escaping Hitler's atrocities will be forced back. That was the official policy. The British didn't implement all their policies and pledges but that particular one was vigorously enforced.

This seemed quite strange to me, since it contradicted their repeated pledges. Being a teenager at that time my impressions were clear: the British Empire joined our mortal enemies, the Nazis, and helped them in their quest to exterminate my people!

I wasn't alone thinking that way, most of my friends believed that as well. After all, as far as we could determine, the evidence was overwhelming.

It wasn't humane behavior, that's for sure. Let's be fair: when you see a crippled human unable to swim, you throw a rope or any other means of support to help avoid drowning. The British, full of praises for themselves about their "fair play" and "human rights," lost their ability to act or help when it came to the Jewish people.

It should be noted that the only reason Britain ruled the land they called Palestine, following the decision by The League of Nations after World War One, **was to help establish a Jewish National Home in the Land of Israel.** That decision came about due to the fact that in time of strife, Jewish people **were not welcome anywhere.** Yet the British violated the spirit of the Mandate and betrayed the League of Nations decision. They introduced their own agenda instead using the excuse that **"allowing more refugees to come will infuriate the Arabs living on the land."** And who are those Arabs the British were so worried about?

Those are the desert scavengers who moved into the Land of Israel as soon as the Roman Empire killed and spread the Hebrews throughout their empire. Those are the descendants of the squatters that nowadays are coming with demands that have no fair legal basis and none whatsoever in factual history.

Hard to believe, you may think, but that's how British politicians behaved during that period. **Foreign Secretary Ernest Bevin did his best to assist belligerent Arabs against the defenseless Jewish population.** Bevin, however, was a known Anti-Semite, so it was definitely normal for him, but then no one in United Kingdom did anything to criticize or stop his one sided policy.

Where were the advocates of even-handed policies?

They were all silent.

In effect they never existed.

The British did not change their acidic ways until the armed Israeli undergrounds (namely: Etzel, short in Hebrew for <u>National Military Organization</u>, and Stern Group, short in Hebrew as Lehi, (full Hebrew name translation: **<u>Fighters for the Freedom of Israel</u>),** came into existence, forcing them to quit and leave since United Nations decision to divide Eretz Israel between Jews and Arabs in 1947. Moreover, it should be noted that the Aronson family of Zikhron-Yaaqov had a pledge from the British authorities to help re-establish a Jewish National Home in the Holy Land if they would provide intelligence to help British troops in the fight against the Ottoman Empire. That's the only reason they provided essential intelligence for the war effort that accelerated General Allenby's decisive victory against the Turks.

The Turkish rulers before that did their best to prevent Jewish immigrants from coming. They imposed laws making it impossible for them to survive. One of the best known laws was in the building of homes. They allowed anyone to build but **destroyed the house by the end of the day <u>if it had n o r o o f.</u>**

In order to outsmart the Turkish authorities the immigrants planted four posts first **completing the roof before the walls.** Thousands built their homes that way before the Turks realized what's going on, and changed the law again to say that the house must be completed, walls and roof, on the same day, to be considered legal. That was a major contributing factor which encouraged support for the British, and their promises. The anti-Turk sentiment enabled the Aronson family to assist with intelligence, thus facilitating a swift decisive British victory.

Sarah Aronson, a thirty year old woman, one of many members of the family, was arrested and accused of spying for the British. The Turkish authorities, in an effort to secure information, tortured her by crushing joints and nerve endings to cause the most pain possible.

Many witnesses said that they heard her blood-curling screams day and night for three days. On the third day she expired. She did not, however, reveal information damaging to the British. Shortly after the war was over, shock hit the local Jewish population like ice-water: the British Government awarded control of Judea's territories west of the Jordan river to Abdullah, the grandfather of the present king of Jordan. Thus, the pledge to the Aronson family was ignored, dismissed as irrelevant. They called the new entity **The Hashemite Kingdom.** It should be noted, however, that no such Kingdom ever existed in the Middle East or elsewhere before they generously gave away chunks of land belonging to another nation.

The British implemented similar unjust, and misleading practices in India, when they followed their "divide and conquer" policy between the Hindu and the Muslim populations. They were in effect the reason for millions dying in bloody clashes as a result. Did anybody hint that the **British leaders should be put on trial as war criminals?** Of course not. Yet, they had the nerve to position themselves these days to play Judge and Jury for others.

The two-faced British policy continued despite **the Balfour Declaration pledge** which promised implementation on their part in the re-establishment of a National Jewish Home. Continuing the duplicity, Tony Blair, the ex-premier of late, now the Quartet Envoy to the Middle-East, confirmed his recommendation that NATO forces should be dispatched to the

Middle-East **to force Israel to make peace with the Palestinians.** Not a word about forcing the Palestinian terrorists to stop rocket launchings into Israeli civilian areas.

Many a time, as premier, he presented himself as a good friend of Israel. I imagine the lip-service was only a political gimmick, like many other British declarations of support. If Blair's advice to send NATO **troops to force Israel to commit suicide** is an indication of being a good friend, then Israel has no enemies – **they are all good friends!**

This is only one of many British expressions of "friendship" towards Israel. Furthermore, British Courts were petitioned to arrest visiting Israeli Military personnel and charge them with "war crimes" against the Palestinians. The alleged "crimes" were the fact that Israel retaliated by using self-defense tactics successfully against Palestinian terrorists.

The Palestinians specifically targeted women, children, and mostly infants. Recently, the British Government recommended a total boycott of Israeli goods from what they consider "occupied" territories. Since when is your homeland occupied territory by the descendants of the **original legal owners of the land?**

In the same vein, what would the British people say if suddenly, out of the blue, should the Irish come with a declaration that England belongs to Ireland? What if they'll maintain that London should be under Irish control? They wouldn't agree, of course, since the Irish never ruled England or London and have no rights to the land. Yet they agree that the Arabs should have their own state within the historical boundaries of the Land of Israel!

Suppose the Irish built a Church in the British capital and invented a legend that an Irish angel went to heaven from there – based on that are they entitled to claim London as theirs? Yet, the British politicians are so anxious to make friends with Muslim countries and agree that because they built a mosque in ancient Jerusalem, the city of David, a known Hebrew king, making up a legend that Mohammed went to heaven from that location, entitles them to claim it all as Arab Land. Someone should remind all Prime Ministers "friends" of Israel, that Britain is no longer ruling the country, United States of America, the waves or the world, and definitely not entitled to tell Israel or anyone else, what to do.

The killing of Israeli children as well as babies followed Yassir Arafat's doctrine who ordered an attack on a northern Israeli nursery. 22 Israeli civilians of all ages were killed, and crippled, mostly children. When questioned by foreign journalists why he attacked children, his answer was blunt: "<u>they grow up and become Israeli soldiers, don't they?</u>" It seems that many British politicians agreed with the position since none of them expressed opposition to such tactics by Islamic Fascists in United Kingdom, or elsewhere. Not in deeds, not even in words.

Blair's successor, Prime Minister Brown, also a declared "friend" of Israel, now demanded that Israel continue to transfer money to Gaza to ease the stress on the Palestinian economy. **This is the first time in history that a sovereign state is urged to finance enemy operations against their own citizens.** Nazi Germany at least was truthful by declaring that their intention was to exterminate all Jews, while the British Government is helping Israel's enemies indirectly to achieve the same, yet still consider themselves Israel's "friends."

CHAPTER ONE

Being eleven years old when Arabs from neighboring villages fired randomly into Zikhron-Yaaqov for no reason at all, was traumatic. The small town situated on top of a mountain in the Shomron mountain-chain faced another mountain giving sharp-shooters a detailed view. The shots shook up the population, instilling fears that more and bigger attacks were on the way.

The town council decided to dig defense trenches around the town, manned by local residents, using weapons from the First World War, namely rifles and old untested bullets, the only weapons and ammunition available. Since the population was under three thousand, including women and children, in order to avoid energy drain, all males from eleven and up, excluding the sick, were assigned to perform guard duties of two-three hours daily.

The training for residents with no gun know-how was short and simple: "load the bullets, aim and squeeze the trigger whenever you think an attack is in the offing." That Friday night, after dark, my turn to stand guard with two other boys of similar age was due.

Shortly after dark a bullet was fired from across the mountain crest. The bullet hissed by at random, hitting no one, slamming into a nearby tree, causing anxiety, rattling nerves all around. This was intended to send a message to whoever provoked us that we were ready to greet them with fire-power. My hands lifted the rifle, inserted a bullet in the chamber and squeezed the trigger as instructed.

The dry click indicated that the bullet failed to ignite. Eight more bullets produced similar results. The ninth bullet ignited, but no one told me that the impact against my shoulder would knock me down.

My fellow guards helped me up, and Rafi was quick to ask, "Is that going to happen every time we use the rifle?"

"I don't know, Maybe something is wrong with my rifle."

Gathering all my courage, the rifle was reloaded and fired again. The bullet ripped into the night creating bouncing echoes as it rushed towards nowhere. At the sound of gun-fire several adults came running to assess the situation. They decided there was no reason to panic: the Arabs probably just wanted to test our resolve.

Two hours later we were relieved by three adults. Yoel, the eldest, asked if the bullet fired at us hit anything.

"Just the tree over there," I said.

"Show me," Yoel requested. Once led to the spot, it took him no time to recognize the hole where the bullet penetrated. Yoel took out his pocket knife and began digging. "Not bad," he said, "the bullet didn't go in deep because of the distance it was fired from." The slug he recovered was almost intact. Close examination by both of us enlightened me. He gave me a valuable lecture about bullets and guns. "When you look at the lead," he explained, "examine the shape."

He went on and explained that when the shape of the lead is completely flattened, it meant that when hitting the target it had lots of power. This implied that it was fired from a short distance. In this case the bullet was fired from a long distance since its power to penetrate was minimal, and the shape almost intact.

"What does this mean?"

"I can tell it's a rifle well maintained."

"How can you tell?"

"The lead has traces of oil."

Not knowing if true, but having no other explanation, his assertion seemed logical. Aware that the rifles we used were from the First World War, poorly maintained, requiring frequent adjustments, cleaning and oiling, gave me the impression that we are definitely amateurs. Furthermore, we had only a limited number of bullets for each gun and few were good enough to ignite when detonated.

"Here," Yoel said," take the rifle home with you and clean it, oil it and do your best to remove all the rust from the inside. Bring it with you tomorrow when you return for guard duty."

Although only eleven going on twelve, my thinking about our situation was to the point: how can we defend the town with a limited number of old guns, and almost no bullets, while our enemies had new weapons, and it seemed, lots of them?

The only way to maintain the balance of power and survive, was to get more and better guns, as well as have more bullets at our disposal. I visited Yoel to show him that the rifle was cleaned and oiled as he suggested, and at the same time, discuss the necessity to acquire better guns and ammunition.

"That's a big problem," he agreed.

"There's a way to get guns fast."

"Really – how?"

"We have to steal them from the British. Or maybe catch some Arabs who use them against us."

He laughed. "Good idea but not as easy as it sounds."

True, easy it was not, in particular that the British were waiting for a chance to confiscate our guns, thus give the Arabs the upper hand. Whether or not anyone stole guns from the Police no one knew, but the British military imposed curfew on the town, and conducted frequent and random searches.

Many of our old rifles were located, confiscated, and their owners arrested. My turn to stand guard again was two days after, and since most guns we used were confiscated by the British, the question was if it made any sense to man the trenches. Apparently that's what the British wanted to achieve: render the town-folks defenseless so that they'll scream for help. Like in the history of the British Empire everywhere: when that happens they come, repel attacks and make the town dependent on their continued rule. However, their intention didn't materialize since by evening we had brand new German guns and some ammunition.

The source was unknown to me but they came right on time because the same evening snipers hit a bigger number of trees than before. This time, we didn't respond. We waited until we could see the shooters should they dare come close enough to be spotted.

During the day my rifle was hidden under the bed. My parents had no idea about it, although they knew about shared guard duty with other boys living in the neighborhood.

Why were the Arabs shooting at the town?

It was unclear to me.

The entire area was dotted with Arab villages. Zikhron-Yaaqov, the only Jewish town around stood out like a sore thumb. Arab extremists apparently believed that they could drive the town-folks out and take their farms and property like they did many times throughout history. This wasn't new: these scavengers remained scavengers for two thousand years. They liked the idea to take by force what others worked for all their lives to develop.

They still do.

The Arabs, or the desert people, did the same thing in ancient history after Judea lost the war against the Romans, and after the last fort, Masada in the Negev, fell into Roman hands. Once the Romans used force to transfer the Hebrew inhabitants to other countries, scattering them throughout the Roman Empire, the homes were left unguarded. Thousands of squatter-scavengers roaming the country came in like locust and devoured the land, consuming, and wasting all they could find.

Judea was known for forests and agriculture at that time. Wild-life was thriving everywhere. After the desert people came in and cut the trees without replacing any, the desert winds covered fertile soil with sand. It didn't take long for the wild-life to disappear: the lions, tigers, and other species that lived on the land. The green fields turned yellow, brown, and vanished. The desert people took over the country completely. The squatters transformed the land of Israel into the biggest desert ever created by man.

They knew that the land didn't belong to them, and should the Hebrews return in the future to claim what was theirs, they may be evicted. Since the land didn't belong to them they didn't care much about it. Destruction became a desired goal.

It still is.

The Palestinians methodically uproot trees only because they were planted by Israelis. There's no consideration that to rejuvenate the soil trees must be planted to help keep desert sands away.

Nowadays, the direct descendants of the desert people, called by the British authorities Palestinians for political reasons, claim the land as their own. These are in effect Muslims claiming the land as Arab land, and therefore, they claim it's theirs. Jerusalem, the city of David, is also theirs, they claim, as though King David was a Muslim. As far as all intelligent people know the City of David was King David's city, and he definitely was no Muslim. In fact he couldn't be since Islam didn't come into existence until much later in history.

The Jewish people were scattered by the Romans around the world ending up in big numbers in Europe. However, the Europeans, did all they could to limit their growth, prohibited Jews from engaging in trade, occupation or any other profession.

That was meant to stifle their growth and keep them as a minority of second class citizens.

The only thing they were allowed to do was trade money. The Jewish people were forced by necessity to save money by skimping on food. Since this was their only permitted occupation throughout the generations, they became financiers and experts in the field. Now, that Jews handled finances, Anti-Semites, looking for scapegoats, accused them of choosing money-handling for the sole purpose of cheating. No matter what the Jews did, they were accused of one thing or another.

They still are.

Baron Rothschild, a Jew, the result of that European policy in France, looked into the situation, and decided to help the Jewish people return to the land, eventually help them become farmers. He bought a huge chunk of land in the Shomrom mountains region, and donated it to Russian and Romanian refugees who immigrated to what was called Palestine at that time. That's how Zikhron-Yaaqov came into existence (translation of the town's name is "Jacob's memory"). The people the baron helped contributed to development of grapes that led to the establishment of the Zikhron-Yaaqov Wine Cellars known worldwide as Carmel Wines of Zikhron-Yaaqov and Rishon Le Zion (a town not far from Tel-Aviv where processing and bottling was the main operation).

In recognition of the baron's generosity his remains were brought to Israel from France. Nowadays the baron's grave site is a well frequented tourist attraction.

CHAPTER TWO

The Arabs, mostly peasants, lived on very limited income: they cultivated a variety of vegetables which were sold to local consumers. The meager income forced them to look for work elsewhere to enable them survive economically.

When Zikhron-Yaaqov was established and prospered, they sought jobs in the grape industry in the fields. Hundreds of them came every morning to work for the local farmers, sometimes bringing their children with them. The very young couldn't get any job, and to pass the time of day, therefore, they befriended local children. We played together and enjoyed each other's company whenever possible.

One of these boys, Ahmed, a ten year old from the village of Fradis, was one of my best friends. We played often, discussed all kinds of topics and exchanged gifts. When the shooting problem began, tension developed. Jealousy developed rapidly into hostility. Resentment fermented and turned into hatred.

It didn't affect the children yet.

However, one morning Ahmed met me in the park in the center of town, greeted me as always, after which we played as usual. Suddenly, with no warning, Ahmed pulled a knife from his pocket, lifted his arm high and tried to stab me in the chest. Since he lifted his arm high enough I managed to catch his hand in midair and twisted it, applying pressure until the knife dropped to the ground.

Picking up the knife, dragging Ahmed into the street, passers-by were informed about what he tried to do. Many others showed up and took Ahmed away. If they called the police or not wasn't public knowledge. Haven't seen Ahmed in town since that day.

Ahmed's hostile gestures was puzzling. Several days Later a report floated around that an Imam, (a religious preacher), visited Ahmed's village, and delivered an inspiring religious message to all. The main message was clear: **death to infidels**, especially Jews. Ahmed listened to the preacher, and like many others, tried to implement Allah's order: **kill the non-believers!**

The next day, children playing in the fields came running, scared and excited. As soon as they reached me, they all spoke at the same time trying to tell me something.

"Slow down – what happened?"

"There's a dead man in the field," David said.

David was a classmate known for a vivid imagination. "How do you know he is dead?"

"His throat was cut and there is lots of blood on the ground."

"You know who the dead man is?"

"Difficult to tell," David explained. "His face and beard are covered with blood. I'm going to call the police. They'll find out."

"Is he old?"

"Yes, very old."

"Before you call the police can you show me where you found him?"

"It's not far. I'll show you."

At the west entrance to town, about fifty yards down into the field, the body of an elderly man lay motionless, sprawled on his back. His eyes were wide open, gazing fixedly at the sky. David was right: the man's throat was slashed. The clotting blood started to jell, clotted, forming a soft crust.

The victim was our town's milk-man. We all knew him. Every morning he made the rounds with his container of milk filling the bottles of his customers. Whether he had a cow of his own or bought milk from his neighbors no one knew for sure. He was the only milkman for many years. Now that extremists pushed for violence against infidels, it was possible that they intended to scare and confuse the town's folk.

First came random shots, now random killing and perhaps additional similar incidents were scheduled for later. Escalating violence via ambushes was always an Arab specialty.

The Arab villagers working in town were quiet people minding their own business. They wanted to keep their jobs, and apparently for that reason they didn't dwell into politics, careful lest they'll jeopardize their livelihood.

Their children, however, grew up and developed into teenagers with constant preaching against infidels by visiting Imams. Apparently, they took the Imams preaching seriously. The realization that the British policy of divide and conquer succeeded once again hit me hard. They instilled in the Arabs the idea that the Jews want to kill them, and at the same time, they tried to instill in the Jewish population fear that the Arabs want to kill them all. However, since nobody wants to die, be it Arab or Jew, hence the conflict intensified, and germs of unrest sprouted everywhere.

Since the milkman was murdered, most people avoided that area, especially after dark. The street at the western entrance to town wiggled close to a valley. An olive grove decorated that field close to the street. During the day one could see if anyone was hiding there. After dark it was impossible to spot a person should anyone be waiting in ambush.

CHAPTER THREE

Due to security concerns as well as the wish to have me attend a better school, my parents decided to make arrangements for me to attend Alliance School on Mount Carmel in Haifa. For a mutually agreed amount of money to cover room and board, I lived in my aunt's house in Kiriyat Motzkin, a suburb of Haifa.

In order to reach the school I had to take a train to downtown Haifa. From there the two hundred stairs walk up to the mountain above carrying the books on my back was no picnic. The books, bulky and heavy, were weighing me down.

Since several other children attended the same school, we all walked together, climbing the stairs and chatting about the taxing walk-up. On the first day a frightening incident that occurred led me to believe that the random shots in Zikhron-Yaaqov weren't as dangerous in comparison. A shot whistling by hit the child on my left. The boy cried loud as he clutched the bleeding wound. Seeing blood covering his shirt sleeve, it seemed obvious to me that the unrest spread throughout the country. Perhaps I was better off staying in Zikhron-Yaaqov.

We all moved to the extreme left in an attempt to make it difficult for a sniper to aim his next shot. The second bullet followed us on the left. It was only by chance that no one was hit this time.

Panic set in.

One of the boys suggested we climb up the stairs in zigzag form to confuse the shooters. Running up the stairs was an exhausting endeavor. We heard voices ricocheting everywhere, in Arabic and in English. Having no time to stop and listen to the barrage of hate loaded bursts, we realized that the curses in Arabic were urging each other to "kill the Jews." Surprisingly, the English version seemed to encourage the Arabs as well. Every time they came close to hit one of the children, the English speaking people applauded, giggled and clapped hands.

When we finally reached the school on that day we had two casualties: one in the shoulder and the second was a flesh wound in the right leg. They were both treated by the school nurse, and that was it. Hushing the incident was apparently school policy to avoid panic among parents.

However, later it became known that the English version originated with two British Police Officers. Instead of trying to stop the snipers they encouraged them on their own or perhaps had instructions to do so. The Police chiefs denied the allegations, of course. When the target practice reached the general public many parents transferred their children to other schools.

For a while the target practice stopped, but then it was renewed every now and then, apparently to not to create a pattern that could be traced. Despite school authorities attempt to keep the situation secret, most children heard about it. Before they could do anything to hush it up, the news spread among parents and children alike as fast as wind driven wild fires.

Myself, as well as most children at that time, harbored no ill feelings to the British presence in our homeland. Incidents like the stairs target practice changed many young minds, including mine. The youth began to look at the British rule as a physical danger to us all. The children, not hostile yet, were encouraged by the British policies to join anti-British organizations.

British policies, intended to suppress Jewish growth, was a major reason contributing to the anti-British sentiment among the younger generation. That's the reason Begin's movement called Irgun Tzvayee Leumi, Etzel for short (National Military Organization in Hebrew) attracted thousands who were anxious to join the ranks. About the same time Lochamey Herut Israel, Lehi for short (Fighters For The Freedom Of Israel in Hebrew) came into existence under the leadership of Avraham Stern, a young Chemist. The British were made aware by Labor Movement zealots about his philosophy and speeches, moved quickly. They arrested twenty one of Stern's followers, in addition to Stern himself. They were sent without trial, to Latroon, a detention camp created specifically to keep the opponents of British policies.

Within a few weeks, all Lehi members escaped and rapidly went underground. The escape was accomplished by digging a tunnel under the camp's fence and exiting on the outside. A series of operations against military and police personnel followed. The authorities issued urgent orders to apprehend and arrest all Lehi members. However, it wasn't as easy as the British wished.

The British failed to apprehend any of them until David Ben-Gurion, later the first Prime Minister of Israel, secretly collaborated with them, supplying them with intelligence leading to his hideout. He did it to gain favor with the authorities, hoping that he'll later be rewarded. As a result, British Police personnel surrounded the house where he was hiding with some of his supporters.

"We know you're there," the police announced. "Come out with your hands up!"

Stern, or Yayeer as he was known by his code name, realized the situation was hopeless, and in order to help his supporters escape, he decided to surrender. While he opened the front door he heard the police commander in charge raise his voice, "If you surrender now peacefully you won't be harmed, I promise!"

Whether Stern believed the promise or not no one could tell, but he raised his arms and came out with his hands up. As soon as he came out, exposed to police firepower, a hail of bullets greeted him. Twenty one bullets blasted his heart, ripping his chest wide open. The hole in his chest was so big even a miracle couldn't save him.

He died instantly.

Apparently that was the intent to begin with. So much for another British promise. The authorities believed that killing the founder of Stern Group was enough to stop Lehi from growing.

However, while they were busy making sure Stern was dead, his supporters escaped using the back doors and windows. By the time the British commander realized that there were others in the house as well, there was no one left to arrest or kill.

The murder of Stern contributed directly to thousands of youngsters joining the undergrounds. From twenty one original members, Lehi reached several thousand. The labor movement stated that only a small number joined Lehi. By lowering the number of Lehi members they hoped to discourage others from joining. The attacks on British Police and Military installations as well as personnel made it difficult for the British to move about as freely as before.

Mines laid on roads British vehicles used exploded, killing some, injuring others in retaliation for British violence against refugees who escaped Hitler's "final solution". Laws against carrying weapons were introduced. The laws were very specific: anyone detained and found to be carrying a firearm or ammunition, would be subject to death by hanging.

About one year following Stern's murder, with Winston Churchill at the helm of the British Government, there were rumors that he planned to dispatch his best friend, Lord Moyne, to Egypt to organize Arab resistance in an effort to trample national aspirations of the Jewish population.

Lehi contacts in England verified that Lord Moyne was already on the way to Cairo. Lehi's Central Command decided that Lord Moyne must be eliminated before he met Arab leaders to organize hostile activities against Jewish towns and settlements.

Two volunteers were needed.

They'd be sent to Cairo to assassinate the Lord before his mission was accomplished. The volunteers were instructed to avoid hurting Egyptian Police or Military personnel at all cost, since that may increase Egyptian hostility against the Jewish population.

The number of volunteers exceeded all expectations. The best were chosen for that operation. The volunteers reached Cairo, rented a hotel room, waiting for the target to come.

They acquired two bicycles, and waited for information about Lord Moyne's traveling plans within Cairo. Soon, they were informed by local sources that the Lord's vehicle will reach a certain area in the afternoon. They bought a detailed map of the city, and had several practice runs to familiarize themselves with local streets. They pretended to be a couple of tourists, holding hands, enjoying each other's company. Since they acted like other Western tourists no one seemed to pay attention to them.

Following a ninety two minute wait, they spotted Lord Moyne's vehicle cruising by. Within seconds, they stopped at a traffic light next to the Lord's vehicle. Without saying a word, they both drew their pistols and fired into the car: the Lord was hit in the head, the body-guard was hit in the chest and the driver was killed as well just as the vehicle began to move when the traffic light changed to green. The vehicle swerved and came to a sudden stop as soon as it crashed into the curb.

Police officers escorting the Lord's car realized what's happening and immediately surrounded the couple attempting to make their escape on the bicycles. Following their instructions not to harm Egyptians they raised their arms when stopped, dropped their weapons and surrendered.

The boys were brought to trial, charged with premeditated triple murder. The Egyptian judge leaned towards life in prison. All they had to do, they were told, was to express regret for the murders, and their life will be spared.

They refused.

The British Government pressured the Egyptian authorities to execute them as fast as possible. They apparently tried to prevent Lehi from trying to rescue them, thus increase chances for what they strived to avoid: international attention.

Since the "regret" suggestion was rejected, the volunteers were urged to ask for mercy from the British Crown instead. If they begged for mercy, they were promised, they wouldn't be executed. All they had to do, the judge pleaded, was ask the British Government to have mercy on their soul.

Again, they refused.

Since they didn't change their mind, they were promptly hung by the neck until dead. With British representatives present and world press following the procedure, everyone everywhere heard and read about it. The attention the British authorities wanted to avoid couldn't be suppressed.

The British plan to encourage a comprehensive attack on all settlements failed. The Arabs remained disorganized although they began their rein of terror. Arab riots against Jews with unofficial British backing in 1936 were in full swing, catching lots of innocents unprepared and vulnerable. Many innocent Jews were murdered just for being Jewish.

British authorities knew they encouraged the hostilities. The idea that Jews were murdered for no reason didn't sit well with the new Israeli generation. Instead of weakening our resolve, these wanton criminal acts by the British toughened us.

CHAPTER FOUR

Due to dangerous developments in the big city, especially cities with mixed populations, my parents decided to bring me back to Zikhron-Yaaqov. On my return it seemed that nothing had really changed: random shots were still fired, every now and then an innocent civilian was murdered for no reason except that he wasn't a Muslim.

The pressure against illegal immigrants as per the British definition increased, so did the operations against them. It came to a point that the British Police and Military, armed with batons, were engaging defenseless refugees physically and hit them in a way an army would use against dangerous enemies. It should be pointed out that their victims were way undernourished and weak, barely able to walk, not to mention fight back.

From the mountains north of Zikhron-Yaaqov one could see the sea shore in direct line of Atlith, a small northern town. Rumors spread fast that a broken down boat with hundreds of refugees was getting ready to come ashore. A company of British Special Forces (or Red Berets as they were called) was rushed to stop them from landing.

The order was specific: stop them at all cost.

Several of my teenage friends, myself included, rushed to our observation post. With the naked eye one could only see people moving about like tiny ants, but little else. Rahamim, a fourteen year old friend, brought his father's binoculars this time. We each had a look at the sea shore.

Following adjustments of the binoculars, I saw clearly Red Berets hitting elderly men, women and children, forcing them back into the boat now stuck in the sand. Many of the refugees fell to the ground, some stopped moving, many moved but were unable to get up. The Red Berets continued hitting their easy prey regardless.

These refugees escaped Hitler's atrocities by miracle. It was clear that they would all die unless immediate help would be forthcoming. Since help didn't arrive most of them were either crippled or died from their wounds.

Later on, the Red Berets, one hundred thousand of them to be exact, were transferred from the Far East to the Land of Israel just for that "dangerous" operation. I doubt whether they were as brave in combat in the Far East against Japanese military units.

Since we couldn't believe our eyes, we decided to go and have a look at the area where the Red Berets battled feeble, weak and under-nourished skeletons. As soon as the last of the British soldiers left, we rushed to see if there was any evidence of what transpired. If we told anyone about what we saw we would be accused of lying or exaggerating.

It took us about one and a half hours to get there. We didn't want to be spotted in that area and be suspected of plotting something. There was no one around but ripples and hills of sand, some torn clothes stained with fresh blood, a few broken dental plates, plus remnants of the wooden small vessel still stuck in the sand.

The sight was enough to convince us that what we saw really happened. What the others felt wasn't clear to me, but my anti-British sentiments were on the rise. The anger made my blood boil and the question was: is that what the British call "fair play?"

Rahamim said, "This is nasty."

"We must stop them!""

"We need training," Samuel declared.

"Training won't help unless we have guns."

We walked back discussing ways to prevent such incidents in the future. Suddenly an idea struck me, "Hey, Rahamim, you had some experience with explosives. Can you put together a road mine, for example?"

Rahamim smiled. "I guess so, but I'm not sure. I never did that before."

"Does your father know?"

"Yeah, he knows. He was an explosive expert in the British Police."

"Great, then you can ask him, can't you?"

Jonathan, a 13 year old boy, living across the street from my parents, said, "Not a good idea, he'll want to know why, wouldn't he?"

"You're right," I agreed.

Rahamim said, "I think I can put together dynamite and wires it in such a way to make it explode, but I'm not sure it will work."

"It's worth a try," was all I said.

"Good, I'll work on it tonight and let you know."

Next morning Rahamim met me after school and was proud of his achievement. "I put together three mines of wired dynamite," he declared. "I'm sure it'll work just like regular mines."

After dark a few of my friends came along to help putting the mines on the road where police cars traveled most. We dug a hole, put the dynamite and the detonator in and covered them with soil.

We planted all three as a test. If they work we'll do the same on the road to the British Military camp between Zikhron-Yaaqov and nearby Benyamina.

After the mines were safe and ready in the ground, Rahamim and I hid up the mountain among the rocks and waited to see if they'll work. We waited almost forty minutes before a squad car drove out of the precinct. Nothing happened despite the fact that we were sure the car drove over two of the mines.

Fifteen minutes later another vehicle drove in, rolling over the third mine. We followed the car to parking. No explosion followed. Frustrated, Jonathan asked, "You sure the detonators are in good working condition?"

Rahamim said, "One hundred percent sure. Maybe the wires got loose."

To find out why the mines failed to explode, we took a chance and snuck to the spot the mines were laid, dug them out and returned to our hiding position. When we reached the illuminated area of the town, curiosity overwhelmed us and we all asked at the same time, "Well, Rahamim, what d'you think is wrong?

"I don't know why they didn't work," he said. "Damn, the detonators are connected and so are the wires."

"I know nothing about mines," I admitted. "Sleep on it, maybe you'll come up with something."

Rahamim slept on it as suggested. He rewired the explosives or so he said and made certain they won't detach. We planted two of the mines in the same spots on the road to the precinct as soon as it got dark enough to proceed. Once again we waited and held our breath when a squad car rolled over them.

The mines didn't explode.

CHAPTER FIVE

Frustration was a strong motivator. We wanted to have effective mines so bad that we'd join the devil to get them. Instead, my friends and I looked for Etzel or Lehi representatives to teach us how to put mines in working order.

The problem was that we didn't know how to reach them.

Studying was always my strongest quest. If I didn't know much about a subject, I went to the local library, selected my subject of interest and absorbed all data found in the instruction books. However, the local library didn't carry books dealing with mines or explosives. Apparently there was no demand for it at that time.

Following several weeks in search of mine instructions we were forced to give up. No one seemed to know anything about the subject. Instead I returned to my prior goal: prepare myself to be accepted by a British College to study Journalism and Creative Writing, my favorite subjects of interest. In order to gain entry to a British College specializing in the above a candidate must have a High School or equivalent diploma. Since my parents had no funds to support my aspirations, I bothered Yona, a disabled neighbor, who had an advanced degree in engineering, plus a vast knowledge of other subjects. Under his guidance, following extensive study of ten to fifteen hours daily Yona felt I could pass the exams of the British Institute in Jerusalem. Once passed, he felt certain, qualifying to gain entry to a College of my choice would be a cinch.

Several years later, back in town with a Diploma in Journalism and Creative Writing, reality hit me hard: very little changed. The British were still in-charge, the terror activities by Arabs intensified. The ranks of Etzel and Lehi grew in numbers, and as a result major operations took place against British Military and Police targets.

Still, no friends knew how to contact representatives of the undergrounds. Monday morning, taking my daily stroll, a thirty five year old man stopped me. This man was one of the original twenty one Lehi founders, who was just released from detention due to terminal illness. He was told that his life expectancy was six to twelve months at the most. Although this man was known to me for many years, his health or political affiliations were not subjects I'd normally be interested in. He was gravely ill. People who knew me advised to avoid contact or even speak to him.

His face was pale, his eyes listless, and when he walked he appeared weak and wobbly. He looked really ill, just like my friends said. His constant coughing attacks made people suspect he had Tuberculosis. He mostly kept to himself, associated with no one, showing no interest in what's going on.

Surprised he stopped and approached me, my assumption was that perhaps he just wanted to be sociable. I changed my mind when his voice lowered to a whisper when he said, "I hear you want to join Lehi, am I correct?"

"How did you know?"

"I've my sources," he said, coughing into his handkerchief

.   "You okay ? Haven't seen you around for years – how are doing?"

"Fine, thank you," he coughed into his handkerchief again, adding, "and how are you doing?"

Shocked to see bloodstains on his white handkerchief, I said, "I'm doing fine, thanks."

"You shouldn't be seen with me," he said in a low voice as he hurriedly returned the handkerchief into his trousers pocket. I'll be brief: if you're serious about Lehi, I can help you join."

"Yes. D'you know how?"

He forced a smile. "Yes indeed. Just talk to a member."

"I have no idea who is a member. D'you know anyone?"

"Yes, of course."

"Where can I find him?"

"You're talking to one."

At first my suspicious mind assumed he was pulling my leg. "You're not kidding me, are you?"

"I don't kid about things like that," he said.

"Okay, what should I do?"

"Nothing. I'll have someone get in touch with you in a day or two. For security reasons, if the contact will ask for your name, it's Giorah."

"Why is that?"

"If you join and are accepted, this will be your code name."

And before I could think of another question, he turned and walked away. That's when my sharply focused eyes spotted a man I never saw before looking me over curiously. Since this man wasn't a local, my first feeling was that he suspected me of something. The possibilities were many: he could be an informer that saw me talking to my sick friend. It could be a Lehi member that will contact me in a day or two or perhaps a double-agent or an undercover detective working for the British.

Two days passed.

Uneasy that no one contacted me despite my friend's promise, doubts surfaced in my mind that perhaps Lehi's Central Command investigated my background, and may have rejected me. On the third day, early afternoon, a young girl, eighteen or so, approached me. She smiled. Her big blue eyes smiled along with her, and that made me more curious than tense. She was definitely not a local. In small towns everyone knew everything about everybody, and Zikhron-Yaaqov was no exception.

Returning the smile, yet wondering about her motives, I heard the soft-soothing voice asked casually, "Is your name Giorah by any chance?"

"Yes. Are you…"

"Yes, I am," she confirmed. "I was supposed to be here yesterday. Sorry I'm late. Is there a place we can talk in private?"

"Sure, we can go to the park."

"Is it far from here?" she asked.

"No, it's over there."

On the way to the park, she said, "My code name is Carmela. From now on if you want to address me use the code name."

"Pleased to meet you, Carmela."

Attempting to figure out why would pedestrians look at me as we entered the park, the first thing on my mind was that they had difficulty believing I landed such a sexy date. Indeed, she was a stunning beauty: blue eyes, dark blond her, slim and medium height. Despite her slim figure she was crafted carefully in the right places. If one of my local friends suddenly dated a girl looking like her it'd have made me curious too, perhaps even jealous.

She led me to a bench in the center of the park, isolated from the others. The closest bench to us was ten to fifteen feet away. She looked at me with fixed piercing eyes, suggesting an unexpected move, "Just for expediency, Giorah, to avoid suspicion, please put your arm around me."

Her suggestion should have satisfied anyone who would think we had in mind anything other than romance. To make it more convincing, my own suggestion was blunt, "To make it more natural, maybe I should I kiss you?"

Smiling, she said, "Slow down, Giorah. Later, if you wish, not now."

"When?"

"Before we part."

Thinking about the prospect of kissing her accelerated my heart beat. She shouldn't have said that. Now all my thoughts concentrated on the kiss at the end.

Looking in all directions we saw people milling around, some were as close as ten feet from our sitting position. "Keep your voice low," was my advice. "They may be trying to listen."

"You're right," she said, her voice as low as possible and yet loud enough to be heard by me. "Why did you decide to join Lehi?"

"I'm not sure. Is it important?"

"Not really. I'm just curious."

"To tell you the truth, it was a tossup between Lehi and Etzel. What's the difference between them, anyway?"

"Etzel is a military organization, acting in big groups. Lehi is more individualized, like a guerilla group, acting in limited cells for security reasons." She stopped talking when a young couple came too close. Shortly after they left, and were over fifteen feet away, she went on, "The basic difference is most important. We all fight for freedom: Etzel believes that the best way to fight the British is destruction of buildings and installations mostly. Lehi believes that the most effective way is to eliminate British military and police personnel."

"Eliminate, you mean, kill them?"

"Yes, they kill us on sight, but not if we kill them first." Considering what she tried to convey, the Bible had something to say about that: "If someone comes to kill you, kill him first," she explained. Thinking it over, I recalled that section in the Old Testament. My eyes looked dreamily ahead. "Does that mean we'll concentrate on individuals?"

"Yes, but only when the individuals act against our national interests."

"Why killing – is there no other way?"

"Not really. The reason being: buildings and installations can be rebuilt quickly using either Jews or Arabs to accomplish that," she said. "This will have no effect on British conduct. If we kill individuals, they not only feel the pain, they'll also have to wait until they are twenty one or so before they can be replaced."

"That's nasty. I don't like that part at all."

"I agree, sure, but that's war."

Running out of questions to ask, I looked her over, trying to clarify all the whys in my mind. Her soft voice asked, "Any more questions?"

"Just one: how do I contact my superiors?"

"You can't. Someone will get in touch with you soon. His code name is Jeremiah. He'll be your direct contact."

"Why d'you use code names?"

"To avoid identification. When the British intercept names in phone conversations it'll make identification much more difficult for them."

Carmela continued and explained that the moment I swear allegiance my life won't be mine. Central Command will decide what I do, where I go, and what operation I can join. If I do not obey, I'll be in trouble. Once I joined I won't be able to quit. Quitting will be like acting against the underground, which is punishable by death.

That part wasn't very encouraging. "You mean once I join I can never quit?"

"Yes, that's correct."

For unknown reasons my lips dried up instantly. Wetting my lower lip with the tip of my tongue, the question erupted, "Why is quitting punished?"

"When you quit you become a danger to us all," she said. "We can't take a chance that you won't sell us out."

Pausing, trying to follow her train of thought, my question seemed to annoy her, "How many were executed so far?"

"None yet. That's because we study the background of all applicants before we talk to anyone. Clear enough?"

"Yes. Can anyone join?"

"No. Recommendation, background, and education are basic first considerations."

"Why education?"

"Anyone can use guns. We've no shortage of action people," she looked around to see if anyone was getting too close. "What we need most are thinkers capable of leading and planning."

Considering what she just told me, it seemed complicated, and definitely more dangerous than expected. To avoid internal conflicts I cleared my throat and asked, "I'd like to think about it. Can I meet you tomorrow to give you my answer?"

She stopped smiling.

"No, you can't. You must decide now."

"That's not fair," I said.

"Why's that?"

"I have other obligations."

"Like what?"

"I've just been appointed regional reporter for The Haifa National Daily."

Her smile returned instantly.

"No problem. You can use your newspaper connections for Lehi's benefit as well."

"I see," I said. "Fine, let's go. I'm ready. What d'you want me to do?"

She said, "Repeat after me: I, Giorah, pledge my life to Lehi and it's rules. I swear to fight our national enemies and sacrifice all for the cause…"

"I, Giorah, pledge my life to Lehi and it's rules. I swear to fight our national enemies and sacrifice all for the cause…" The pledge went on at length about obedience, sacrifice and dedication.

Carmela listened attentively as I repeated word by word and summarized it with a smile.

"Now you can kiss me if you still wish."

Trying to kiss her on the lips was futile because she quickly turned the left cheek to me. The kiss touched the cheek instead.

"This was no kiss!"

She laughed. It sounded like a short-fuse giggle. "That's the best I can do," she said."

"Can I ask you a question?"

"Depends. Go ahead."

"What if I violate the pledge?"

"You'll be asking for trouble."

"I can deny I ever pledged anything, can't I?"

She laughed. "Won't do you any good."

"Can you prove I did?"

"Yes, of course. My tiny recorder is proof enough – don't you think so?"

Taken aback, I said, "That's sneaky. You don't look like a sneaky girl."

Her smile widened. "Looks can be misleading, Giorah," she said. "Remember that!"

"So, I'm on the hook – is that it?"

"Yes, you are. Enough questions, I really must leave."

"Can I ask you only one more question?"

"One, no more - what is it?"

"Will I see you again?"

"I don't think so," she said, adding, "remember, your direct contact is Jeremiah, not me."

"Will Jeremiah introduce me to the other members in town?"

"No. Each cell has four or five members only."

"Why is that?"

"Just in case a member is captured by the British, if he's tortured he cannot endanger all members, only the ones he knows."

"That means I'll have no contact with others, correct?"

"I've no idea. It depends on circumstances."

"What circumstances?"

"That's enough, no more questions," she said and glanced at her wrist-watch. "I've to leave now."

"What's the rush?"

"No rush," she smiled wide, the dimples on her cheeks deepening. "Someone is supposed to pick me up in twenty minutes."

"It'll seem funny to people who saw us to see you leave all of a sudden, at least let me walk you into the street."

"That's just fine," she said. "Don't feel bad, Giorah. I wish I could stay. I can't."

"Nice meeting you, Carmela," I said. "I expected you to be a man, though."

"Male chauvinist, aren't you?"

"Not really," I corrected. "But, after all, it's a man's world, isn't it?"

"I agree, but now I must say goodbye, Giorah. Good luck."

Luck, however, was in limited supply.

My contact ordered me to organize a training program for several local cells. Experts from the outside were scheduled to come and instruct us about light arms, machine-guns, mines assembly etc. Since Central Command planed several major operations it was essential that all cell members be familiar with the use of all weapons available.

Being familiar with most caves around the mountain crest, my recommendation centered on the biggest cave in the outskirts of town. Together with an outside instructor our total number reached thirteen. We were taught how to handle guns, ammunition and how to assemble and activate mines.

Superstition indicated that number thirteen would bring bad luck. Never before superstition, but what followed almost made me a believer. The training sessions in the cave were hectic. We were so busy with the instructions that we neglected to examine the presence of tiny black bugs roaming around. The problem was that the bugs attacked wherever they found exposed skin. Most of the bites concentrated around the ankles. Since they couldn't fly, the ankles seemed to be the highest they could reach.

The bites caused itching, irritation and distraction. All men present scratched the bitten areas to the extent that the ankles looked like raw meat. The scratching enabled the bug venom to circulate faster. Describing the bugs to a medical student, a friend of mine, he suggested that in his opinion the best way to get rid of them was to spray the cave and the bugs with lots of DDT.

Once we sprayed the bugs with DDT we couldn't use that cave any longer: we probably angered them to extreme. Instead of eliminating them, biting accelerated. Within a few days weakness and aches took over every part in my body. All cell members, including the instructors, developed similar symptoms. Doctor Bear, the local doctor, considered an excellent physician, tried to help but the symptoms overwhelmed him. He never encountered anything like it. He drew blood, ran a few tests and concluded that the condition indicated a rare kind of disease: **Reoccurring Tropical Malaria.**

Reoccurring Tropical Malaria, according to history, was rampant in United States during the civil war as well. It caused big problems in USA at that time as well since Quinine pills, which were normally used against regular Malaria, had no effect on Tropical Malaria victims.

Unfortunately, Doctor Bear declared there's no medication against that type of malaria. In order to stop the spread of that rare Malaria he decided to take a chance and inject me with two shots of **Arshernomine,** known as **Salvarsan,** ordinarily used as a powerful anti-biotic intended to eradicate Syphilis. The drug, not in use any longer, was replaced as soon as soon as penicillin was introduced in 1940.

Good riddance since Salvarsan had an arsenic base. If that fact was publicly known it might have scared a novice to death. The idea was that if these shots were powerful enough to cure Syphilis, they might help alleviate Tropical Malaria as well.

Having no idea what's involved Doctor Bear was authorized by me to go ahead. The first shot into the right upper part of the leg was supposed to kill the bacteria, and eliminate spreading. The second shot, two weeks later, according to Doctor Bear, would clean the blood stream of the toxins injected. The predictions didn't work as the well as the good doctor promised.

However, having no idea about the possible effect of that potent drug, suspicion that my bad luck caused it all was a possibility. After the second shot, almost immediately, my body felt so weak that long periods of rest to regain my strength was necessary. My vision was so blurred I couldn't see my way around. My eyes began to hurt, and when I looked into the mirror, shock gripped me: instead of two normal looking eyes I faced two red balls of fire, apparently the result of busted vessels.

Doctor Bear was notified.

Rattled by the effect, he came running with his black bag. He examined me from all sides, took blood pressure, asked me to cough, take a deep breath, and shake his hand. The blood pressure was very high, the coughing was weak, the deep breath was shallow, and the shaking of his hand proved that my muscles were too weak to squeeze.

The doctor was confused.

He never encountered a similar situation, and it was clear he had no idea what to do. To be on the safe side, he gave me several pills to swallow. If there's no improvement, he suggested a visit to his office in a week or so. He instructed my mother to give me nourishing foods, lots of fruits, and encourage vigorous exercise.

Within a week I was weaker than before. The visit to the doctor's office, even though he was located within walking distance, was out of the question. Instead, the doctor came to visit me again. After examining me, he suggested more nourishing foods and fruits to rebuild my strength.

Fever attacks were frequent amid excessive sweating. The fever overwhelmed me, but at the same time, the feeling of winter frost penetrated every fiber in my body. Shivering and sweating lasted for hours. Repeated attacks that followed drained all the energy from my aching body, rendering me unable to do anything productive. The big quantities of nourishing foods and fruits didn't help much. The food was supposed to help regain lost energy. Frankly, it didn't improve my condition. Weight loss continued despite the enormous quantities of foods consumed. Chewing so much only made my jaws ache. At the end of three weeks, after a meal, I tried to bite into an apple as recommended by the famous saying that **"an apple a day keeps the doctor away",** but it didn't work either. Maybe the saying should be changed to **"an apple a day brings the doctor your way."**

Biting once into the apple caused a frightening condition: I couldn't open my mouth to dislodge it. The left side of my body, the entire length from the eye, nose all the way down to the toes, was completely immobilized.

That's when panic set in.

The problems multiplied to the point of desperation. My parents seemed anxious to help, tried to force me to have chicken soup thinking it was **"the Jewish penicillin"** many believed it to be. When the soup didn't help either, they gave up.

Doctor Bear was summoned once again.

He rushed over, his eyes and face clouded with worry. He realized apparently that the arsenic-based drug wasn't the answer, and if I join my ancestors it would be bad for his reputation. He might even be charged with negligence or malpractice. Maybe even murder.

Following another long examination he declared that there's nothing he can do about the paralysis. He recommended a trip to Tel-Aviv, check into a hospital equipped to treat me with shots of penicillin to fight the paralysis. However, penicillin was new at that time, and its effect wasn't really known. There was no guarantee it'll work, or even if it'll not aggravate the condition.

Nurses in the Hospital injected me with big dosages of penicillin shots hourly for several days. It seemed that my entire body was full of holes due to the shots. Perhaps drinking liquids should be avoided lest they'll come out like a spray through the broken skin.

On the eighth day, the paralysis gradually subsided. When asking medical experts for explanations, no one could to tell what cured me, why and how. But none of them revealed that the arsenic based Salvarsan could have been the culprit. Doctors, lawyers, and many experts, were always reluctant to raise doubts about their colleagues. That could be the reason.

For several months after my return home, I was forced to consume nourishing foods plus plenty of fruits whether my taste buds liked it or not. The paralysis was almost gone, while the weakness and physical aches diminished considerably. The eyes, red balls of fire only weeks ago, returned to normal as well.

That painful experience convinced me that doctors don't know as much as it's believed. That's the reason physicians call it the practice of medicine. If they knew everything as many of us thought they should, they won't have to practice, they'll know exactly what they're doing. Apparently physicians believe that experience is the best teacher **so** that they will continue to practice to the end of time.

That taught me that when encountering a physician that admits he wasn't certain, we shouldn't trust him blindly as many of us do nowadays. Perhaps asking for a second opinion would be in order. The price of this lesson was almost fatal, enough to shake your belief in medicine.

CHAPTER SIX

Underground operations were carried out against police stations, military camps and installations. Zikhron-Yaaqov region couldn't participate in any of them due to jurisdiction restrictions. However, we asked for additional mines since we had only two. They were assembled and ready, unlike the crude mines my friends attempted to put together several years ago.

A week later three more mines were added to our arsenal. There was no indication why our needs were addressed so fast. In addition to the mines, we also received a big supply of machine-gun ammunition to have ready for action in time of need.

Unexpectedly, an urgent order from Central Command hit us: the British military dispatched reinforcements by train to stop all attempts by refugee boats to land. Additional Red Berets were rushed over from Cairo, Egypt. Troops were estimated to be two thousand. Since the tracks ran through Benyamina and Zikhron-Yaaqov on the way to Athlit, where immigrant boats usually landed, all Lehi cells in the area were ordered to figure out ways to stop the reinforcements from reaching their destination.

The train had to pass through a section of the terrain situated between two steep hills. We decided that would be the best place to plant the mines. Now we had the mines, the wires, detonators and the personnel to plant and operate them.

There was no problem there.

There was danger, though: the British military camp was so close to that area it could probably prevent us from planting the mines on the rails during daylight hours. The train, however, was scheduled to reach the hilly area at noontime the next day. For that reason we waited until seven PM when darkness took over in order to plant and secure all necessary equipment.

By eight thirty PM all five mines were in place.

The space between them was calculated so that they'll cover the entire length of the train. The wired mines could be activated from the top of the hill by remote control. We planned to do it so that when the first and last car will effectively enable the destruction of all cars. Moreover, to make certain that most Red Berets will be eliminated, we positioned two machine-guns to hit the beginning of the train as well as the last cars. The machine-guns, we figured, will be activated in case hostile fire will be aimed at us by escaping Red Berets on the ground.

The terrain, mostly rocks, low bushes and weeds, was dry during the summer, but then we faced the winter season. The rains during the winter months were sporadic, but when they came they lasted a long time, sometimes days. In that case the ground will be wet, probably muddy. That will enable British investigators to follow our tracks.

The tracking advantage the British had worried me most. We knew that the police had trained dogs to assist them track and determine in what direction we retreated after the operation. If they knew where we came from, curfew will be imposed. Curfews were usually used to detain all civilians in the operation area. Their next step was an effort to separate the underground members from others. As a rule they arrested on sight any male from fifteen up who cultivated a moustache. Where they got that idea, no one knew. Many Lehi members had no moustache, and for that reason they were never detained or suspected.

Since a medium size moustache decorated my lips, it meant possible detention. To counter the possibility of being tracked, we secured an adequate supply of hot pepper in powder form. We didn't know whether this will do any good, realizing we had only hope and prayers on our side.

About seven fifteen PM in the evening, we reached the spot that would enable us control the operation. The mines were planted as planned. The wires were connected along with the detonators. It wasn't an easy feat because we couldn't use flashlights lest the guards in the British military camp below may suspect something fishy, and rush over to investigate.

By eight thirty five PM everything was ready to go.

Next morning we reached the ambush position about eleven o'clock. Getting there was our biggest drawback since the British sentries might detect our movements. The drawback was that as soon as the operation will start, the explosions will alert them, possibly seal our escape route. However, since it was close to lunch-time, the guards, we hoped, would be thinking more about their stomach needs.

At eleven forty six the sound of an approaching train reached us. It was too early for the Red Berets to arrive, but then the British may have had detailed intelligence about our plans, perhaps decided to change the scheduled time.

The machine-gun operators as well as myself, plus one more cell member at the detonator lever, were on alert. Tension gripped my chest, while the mouth turned so dry it forced me to lick my lips to avoid excessive dryness.

The rumbling sound of an approaching train turned louder.

The lump in my throat grew bigger.

Whether it was the result of fear or anxiety wasn't clear. The fear that something might go wrong dominated my thoughts. Warning my cell members to get ready but avoid doing anything without my specific say so, we were ready for whatever may develop. Hoping it was the military train we expected, not a regular passenger train, was our biggest worry.

As soon as the first car pushed forward along the tracks we realized it was a freight train moving leisurely along. It was a very long train with two locomotives providing the power. From our position we saw agricultural supplies as well as equipment. From time to time the metal wheels clicking against the tracks hit me hard. What if the weight of the train accidentally triggered one of the mines?

Five to ten minutes later the last car gradually disappeared with the increasing distance. The metallic sound of wheels hitting the tracks gradually stopped. As soon as the train was no longer a danger, tensions eased. The lump in my throat gradually dissolved the anxiety almost to the point of relaxation.

It was already after twelve o'clock noon.

The Red Berets' train was scheduled to arrive within half an hour. To avoid tension's return, smoking came to mind. Lucky, none of us smoked. Smoking during an operation was against underground rules anyway. Besides, if any of us did smoke, the sentries in the camp may notice the cigarette smoke as it whirled upward, perhaps prod them to investigate.

Soon it was twenty to one PM.

Tensions returned as soon as the sound of train wheels of a second train approached the position of the mines. There was no time to think of anything else but the mission at hand. We hoped and prayed that the mines would explode as expected, but should they fail, what then?

All three cell members looked at me for instructions. When the first car reached about ten feet before the first mine my arm was ready to give the signal. Within seconds the train was in the proper position. Raising my voice, hoarse and strained, the order was automatic, **"N o w!"**

The lever was depressed. Every second felt like minutes. Fear of failure dominated my thoughts. When we were ready almost to give up, three successive explosions rocked the mountain top. The noise hit my eardrums with a deafening force creating a symphony of sound ripples within my inner ears. The sounds lasted no more than a minute, but they were so loud that rattling shockwaves vibrated freely, pushing for a headache.

Looking down at the train wreck, screaming and cursing in English reached us. Immediately after the angry curses shots were fired in our direction. Our own gunners manning the machine-guns opened fire in successive bursts until the British fire stopped. The cursing ceased as well. Moans and groans filled the air instead with occasional muffled screams intermingling.

Having no idea whether the Red Berets were completely eliminated, I felt a little shaky. Suspecting should the mission be considered a failure, I'd probably be blamed for it, since my contact entrusted me with the execution of the operation.

Taking the blame for failure wasn't a good start.

Dismantling the equipment, and carrying it with us to a nearby cave, kept us busy for a while. We walked slowly, making certain we bent low enough to avoid detection.

While carrying the equipment we spread pepper powder on our tracks. The pepper powder should force the dogs, if they brought any, to sneeze. The pepper was so potent it forced me to fight the inclination to sneeze. Assuming the sniffing dogs would loose their ability to track we'd be in the clear. If they didn't that might be the end of us. We knew from prior experiences that if they'd find us they'll shoot to kill first and ask questions later.

Later on, in order to fulfill my journalistic obligation to Haifa Daily, contacting the Police Precinct was a must. The desk sergeant said, "Police_Department. Can I help you, sir?"

"I'd like to speak to Inspector Johnson, please."

"Who should I say is calling, sir?"

"This is Haifa Daily Regional reporter."

Several clicks later a thick voice came on the line, "Inspector Johnson here," he said.

"This is regional reporter for Haifa Daily - I heard explosions, inspector – can you tell me what's happening?"

The hesitation in his voice revealed that he didn't know much himself. "As far as I know a group of vicious terrorists attacked a train carrying Military personnel."

"Was the train derailed?"

"I've no details yet," he said. "I was about to drive to that location – if you like, you can join me. I always cooperate with the press."

"Thanks, inspector, I'd like to join you. I can reach the station in half an hour."

"No need for that," the inspector said. "I'll have a squad car pick you up. Wait at the entrance to the park."

"Thanks, inspector."

"See you soon," he said, and with that he hung up the phone.

Twelve minutes elapsed before a squad car cruising along came to a gradual stop by the entrance to the park. The driver, a uniformed police officer, opened the window and asked, "Are you the reporter I'm supposed to pick up?"

"Yes, that's me."

"Hop in quick. Inspector Johnson is waiting," he said.

The inspector didn't wait long.

Within ten minutes we reached the police fort, a stone building designed to sustain heavy weapons penetration when attacked. Inspector Johnson waited with his driver in another squad car with the engine running.

"Nice to meet you, inspector," and entering the squad car, now ready to go, the inspector didn't even look at me. He merely nodded and continued to give the driver instructions which route to follow.

Finally, he turned and explained, "If we get there too early we may interfere with the ambulances and medical personnel."

"I'm in no rush, inspector."

"If we get there through the Benyamina side, we may be able to get in, I believe."

Benyamina was south of Zikhron-Yaaqov, but in my estimation we'd interfere with the medics since there was no other way to reach the tracks. Meantime Inspector Johnson filled me in reference to the extent of the casualties.

"I have no numbers yet," he said. "As far as I heard, the casualties are heavy." He went on and said that he's glad to have a reporter escort him to witness the murderous ways of the terrorists that don't care at all for human life.

"Where were the troops going, anyway?"

"They received orders to stop immigrants from landing in the area," he stated.

"Stopping, how: shoot them?"

"No, of course not. We don't do things like that," he said.

Knowing the question will upset him, pressing on came next, "Clobber them, or what?"

"We don't hit people unless they use violence against us."

The inclination to tell him that I witnessed many a time British troops do just that, even if the refugees were so weak they couldn't even walk, let along resist, was very strong. He may turn hostile if the questions turned critical. After all, his cooperation was essential to verify that the operation was a success.

Soon we reached the scene.

Dozens of medical personnel carrying blood stained Red Berets, loading waiting ambulances to capacity, moved back and forth, cursing and giving instructions. A big number of Red Berets were motionless. They decorated the ground, blending into the terrain surface with the dull green of their uniforms. Their bodies, covered with blankets, led me to believe they were all dead.

Though satisfied the operation was a success, my feelings were mixed: sadness that so many humans, even if they were enemy soldiers, had to suffer as a result, pressed heavily on my conscience.

What was I talking about?

It just sunk in: we were enemies, after all. Our interest was to chase them out of the Eretz Israel (in Hebrew: the Land of Israel). Their interest was to kill us on sight, thus serve the British interest by helping the Arabs. Moreover, they had orders to shoot us. When given the chance, we had orders to kill them. That's the way wars were conducted since the beginning of time, wasn't it?

CHAPTER SEVEN

The train operation, as suspected, brought on curfews for Zikhron-Yaaqov and Benyamina. The British authorities couldn't determine the area underground members came from, although they brought dogs to track us. As anticipated, they couldn't sniff much with pepper-powder in their noses.

The curfews included searches at random locations. They didn't produce results. Once the pepper-powder confused the dogs, it was impossible to pinpoint anything. In order to make sure that no clues were left for the British military to hang on, closer inspection of the train operation site to examine tracks, if any, seemed important to me so that we may avoid errors of the same sort in the future.

Reaching the area on foot wasn't easy. Although it wasn't far, it wasn't around the corner either. As I was looking around a demanding strange voice hit my ears. "Don't move," the voice was calm but decisive.

Not knowing what's the problem, obeying seemed to be the only way. The same voice ordered me to turn around. Facing three British officers from the military base downhill, tension pressed against the lungs to the point of depression: one was a Captain, the other two were First and Second Lieutenants. All three had pistols pointing towards my chest with itchy trigger fingers, fixed eyes, and threatening postures.

"What's the problem, Captain?"

The same voice, ignoring my question, asked, "What are you doing here, sir?"

"I'm representing Haifa Daily," my explanation was brief. "I believe that's the spot the terrorists operated from – didn't they?"

The Captain's attitude indicated that he didn't trust me. His trigger finger tensed as he asked, "How did you know?"

"I'm not sure. I thought this to be the best site for an ambush."

The Captain looked at me, his eyes scanning my pockets, looking for bulges. He asked, "May I see your ID, please?"

In order to access my wallet to show him my Press Card, my hand reached for my pocket. I froze again when the Lieutenant on the Captain's right raised his voice, "Hold it, don't make any sudden moves, sir."

"I just want to show you my ID card, Lieutenant."

"Take it out slow and easy."

The wallet contained several cards, and after flipping through, the Press Card was in plain view. "Here, Lieutenant, is it okay to give it to you?"

The Lieutenant didn't respond. He grabbed the Press Card from my hand and gave it to the Captain. The Captain looked it over, whispering into the ear of the officer on the left. Examining the card once more, the Captain returned it, his eyes scanning the pocket which contained the wallet on the right, plus numerous notes on the left.

"D'you have anything else that can verify your identity?" Still, the Captain was suspicious. Anyone, apparently he believed, could carry a Press Card, even an official ID and still be a terrorist. "Sorry, that's not good enough - can anyone verify that you're a reporter for Haifa Daily, sir?"

"If you call my Editor he'll tell you who I am, I'm sure - would you like his phone number?"

The Captain didn't like my answer. He asked , "Where d'you come from?"

"Zikhron-Yaaqov."

"What are you doing in Zikhron Yaaqov?"

"I live there."

"Can anyone there vouch for you?"

"Yes, of course. You can call the Police and speak to Inspector Johnson. He knows me."

"Fine," he said, "Let's go to the base, then."

Down the base, being led into a spacious office the First Lieutenant pointed to a nearby chair. "Please sit down, sir."

The Captain said, "We can find out exactly who you are if what you say is true."

"I have no reason to lie."

Ignoring my statement, he lifted the phone, dialed a number and said, "This is Captain McGregor from the military base. May I speak to Inspector Johnson, please."

The only thing my ears picked up from my sitting position were phone clicks. The Captain, tense and formal, waited about a minute before he heard a voice responding. "Yes, this is Captain McGregor, is this Inspector Johnson?" Apparently Inspector Johnson verified. "D'you know the regional reporter for Haifa Daily?" Unable to hear the answer, my nerves turned jittery. Hoping the inspector vouched for me, my chances of getting out of trouble will be best. The Captain's voice vibrated, "Yes, of course. The captain pushed the phone into my hand watching me lift the receiver to my ear. "Inspector Johnson here – what's the problem?"

"I was detained when I inspected the hill…"

"Don't worry, Captain McGregor suspects everybody," the inspector said. "Let me talk to him."

Returning the phone to the captain, waiting for the next step, my ears strained. Captain McGregor exchanged a few words with Inspector Johnson, returning the receiver to the cradle.

"Captain, did he vouch for me?"

"Yes, he did."

"Am I free to go?"

"Of course. I apologize. Ever since the train attack we must be very careful, sir."

"Thanks, Captain."

"Lieutenant Mathews will take you back where we found you to finish your site inspection," he said.

"I appreciate that. Thanks again."

"How did you get here, sir – on foot or you drove a car?"

"On foot. It isn't very far."

"When you complete your inspection, Lieutenant Mathews will drive you to Zikhron-Yaaqov."

"It's not necessary."

"I insist, sir."

"That'll be nice, Captain, thank you."

Lieutenant Mathews fulfilled the Captain's promise. He escorted me to the area where they found me. Looking around, trying to impress my escort that my interest was solely with reference for the purpose discussed, I waved and walk out. Half an hour later Lieutenant Matthews escorted me to his jeep and drove cautiously north to Zikhron-Yaaqov. Since the curfew failed to produce results, the British changed tactics: they detained all males walking the streets with a moustache. For reasons unknown, the British suspected that all "terrorists" in addition to moustaches had brown Semitic eyes.

Since my daily walk on Main Street was at full swing when Police sweeps materialized, I was detained as well. Trying to explain my journalistic status was merely a waste of time. No one listened.

Close to three thousand males were detained on that day from both towns. Loaded into buses, and trucks, the military transported us all to Latroon, a detention camp created specifically for the purpose of handling political suspects. No reason was given for the detention. No information was disclosed whether it's a mass arrest awaiting trials, or merely a temporary detention with no end in sight.

As soon as we reached the destination, all suspects were herded into several groups. In order to make it easier for British interrogators, the groups were mixed with people from both towns. The theory behind it was that if we don't know each other it will be easier to press us to admit that we are the "criminals" they wanted us to be.

British detectives decided to separate the ones who spoke English and those who spoke Hebrew only. They asked the English speaking men to move to the right. The ones that spoke Hebrew were instructed to move to the left. Since my language skills included both languages, I hesitated.

The lead detective explained, "English to the right, Hebrew to the left – what are you waiting for?"

"I speak both English and Hebrew."

"English to the left," he said. "How well d'you speak English?"

"Fairly well, I have a degree in Journalism from a British College."

"You're a reporter, then?"

"Yes, I work for Haifa Daily"

Being a reporter didn't impress them at all, neither did they grant me any leeway. The English speaking men were scheduled to be interrogated first.

Being among the first to be interrogated we were directed to a spacious room, told to sit by a long wooden table, facing five detectives barking questions in rapid succession. They wanted to know where I was on the day the train was attacked, if any witnesses can prove my alibi and whether my profile included a criminal record. Next was the question whether arrests, if any, were for either violent or non-violent crimes.

"I was never arrested."

"Never?"

"Yes. I'm a law-abiding citizen."

The lead detective, a tall blonde man with a pasted smile, answering to the name of Rodney, looked at me with his glowing dark blue eyes and said, "Now that we know who you are, it would help if you tell us why you chose to study English."

Astounded, not knowing if the answer will help detective Rodney prove anything, I said, "I always wanted to be a newsman, so I studied journalism in a British College."

"How come a British College?"

His intention was to trick me into admitting that studying the English language was merely a cover for my anti-British feelings.

"English is a second language in The Land of Israel."

"You mean Palestine, of course."

"You call it Palestine, I don't."

The detective paused for a minute or so, looked me over, and asked, "Who paid for your college tuition – you belong to any organization?"

"I don't belong to any organization."

"Did your parents pay your College tuition?"

"No, sir. My parents couldn't afford it."

"If no organization paid the tuition and your parents couldn't afford it, who did?"

"I did."

"Where did you get the money for it?"

"I got a job washing dishes in restaurants on my free time. That paid my bills."

Silence prevailed for about five minutes as the detectives discussed the answers among themselves. They seemed suspicious that I had fitting answers no matter what they asked. When the discussions were concluded, Detective Rodney looked at me in silence. Finally, he said, "Fine for now. We may get back to you later on. Any objections?"

"None whatsoever."

Ignoring my explicit answer, he said softly, "You'll be assigned to group number one. You'll be in charge. If anyone misbehaves, you are responsible. Is that clear?"

"Yes, sir.

"Any questions?"

"Yes, why me? I have no experience supervising people."

"You speak English well. That's an advantage. Any more questions?"

"One more question."

"Go ahead, sir."

"How many people in a group?"

The pasted smile widened. "Five to six hundred, no more."

Thank God for little miracles. The number could have been higher. Being unaware, though, what will happen if anyone in my assigned group will misbehave or escape, I couldn't figure out what to say. The possibility, though, worried me. I didn't elaborate or argue for fear they would resent my digging nature.

Group number one was assigned to a series of long wooden structures containing beds military style. Each bed had a number and the occupants will be referred to by the number on allocated beds.

Since the persons in my group were called in for interrogation one by one, being present during their questioning wasn't possible. Requesting to be present will arouse their suspicion, perhaps ask questions that should be kept secret. The detectives chose one of the English speaking detainees to act as translator for non-English speaking suspects. If they wanted me to be present they would have chosen me, wouldn't they?

Within a period of two weeks all detainees were identified, questioned and assigned to numbered beds. None were found guilty belonging to a terrorist organization. For that reason about half of the suspects, including myself, were released. I didn't know about the others, but I was forced to provide my own transportation back to Zikhron-Yaaqov, and it wasn't cheap.

Back in circulation, Central Command instructed that all cells throughout the land should increase their activities against British Police and military personnel. Having no idea how exactly the cells in the rest of the country implemented the order, didn't help me decide what to do. In my area the decision was to concentrate on individuals. British Police personnel used to come into town whenever they felt like having alcoholic beverages. Our specific announcement that no British police officers or military men coming into town were welcome. Violators will be treated like enemies. All vacant walls carried pasted English messages warning British personnel to stay away.

As a result my cell members detained a nineteen year old police officer in town and brought him to trial according the underground's standing orders. Our intention was to harass and frighten off individuals from developing friendly relations with the locals, thus prevent them from gathering intelligence that might be used against underground members.

We took the young policeman to a deserted hut out of town where no one could interrupt. First came the questioning by the three of us, considered judges, to determine the degree of criminal guilt. Seniority entitled me to ask the first question,

"Your name, please."

"John Mcdormit, sir."

"How old are you, John?"

"Nineteen, sir."

He looked terrified.

Judging by the way he watched every move I made it was obvious he feared for his life. His fixed stare concentrated on my face as though he hoped to soften my attitude. He avoided, though, direct contact with my eyes.

"When did you join the Police Force?"

"Five months ago, sir."

"Why the Police Force?"

"I needed a job."

"There are other jobs, why this one?"

"The Government ad stated **join the Police Force and see the world. Excellent conditions.** I believed it."

"You still believe that?"

"No, sir."

"D'you hate the Jewish people, John?"

"No, sir."

"Should your Commanding Officer tell you to shoot us, you will, correct?"

"I don't know, sir, no one told me to do that."

The member on my left whispered in my ear suggesting to speed-up the procedure and get it over with. Without responding to the suggestion, the questioning continued.

"Did you know you're not allowed to come to town?"

He seemed stunned. "No, sir."

"Well, since you belong to our enemy forces, you cannot come into town, not for a drink, contact with locals or any other reason. D'you know that?'"

"No one told me that. sir."

"You heard about our rules?"

"No, sir."

"Now you know."

John hastened to say, "I won't come from now on, sir."

"Too late, John, you already violated our rules – do you admit that?"

"Yes, sir, but it won't happen again."

"I appreciate your promise," my eyes looked straight into his. "But, since coming into town is a criminal offense, you're now on trial and will be punished severely."

He wet his lips, hesitated for a split second, his lips moving as though he wanted to say something. Apparently he reconsidered and said instead, "Yes, sir."

"Your offense is punishable by death - did you know that?"

"No, but I'm very sorry, sir," he mumbled, his lips quivering slightly, his eyes shifting from one to the other. "I didn't know any of that, sir. I didn't violate your rules on purpose, therefore, I don't believe I'm guilty."

Gaby, the cell member on my left, cleared his throat. He said, "I'm quoting what your British Courts always reminds us all, John: **ignorance of the law is no excuse."**

"Yes, sir."

The three of us consulted each other in whispers. John followed every move we made, shifting his leg position from time to time. Gaby raised his voice and said, "John Mcdormit, we, the judging panel, found you guilty as charged."

Before John had a chance to protest, I said, "In our legal judgment you deserve the death penalty." John lowered his eyes, this time his hands quivered along with his lips.

"You will…kill me, sir?"

Ignoring his question, my legal summary continued, followed by a warning. "However, by a majority of two to one we decided to dismiss the case against you only with a warning instead to all British personnel in the Police Fort: death penalty awaits any of you who comes into town for any reason."

The quivering gradually stopped. I heard his hoarse voice say, "Thank you, sir."

"Remember the verdict."

"Yes, sir."

"This time you're free to leave."

John didn't wait even a second. Without waiting for my reaction he breezed out of the hut and disappeared into the distance.

Before I could relax and concentrate on other chores, the news that a fifteen year old boy, member of Lehi, was caught pasting the Lehi wall-papers. He was quickly brought before a British Judge. The boy was sentenced to fifty lashes in public. Whether this particular boy could survive such punishment was doubtful. Considering that it was harsh and dangerous for an adult, it definitely was too much for such a young fragile body.

Word reached me that Lehi's Central Command felt the same way. Determined to prevent the first lashing of the land, Geula Cohen of Lehi, declared in the underground Radio broadcast that should the British Police go ahead with the lashes, the underground will be forced to do the same to British Police personnel in public. The same warning was printed in Lehi wall-papers and pasted everywhere.

The threat to retaliate with lashes for lashes wasn't treated seriously. No one believed that Lehi could implement the threat even though it fit the Biblical definition of "an eye for an eye."

The boy was lashed publicly in Nathanya's public square with a crowd of hundreds watching as he collapsed numerous times. Whenever he collapsed, officers propped him up, secured his body with ropes so that the punishment could continue. The sentence was carried out to the finish regardless of flowing blood, screams and moans.

Every time the boy collapsed due to the painful lashes he was propped up. The lashes continued despite the boy's screams, as well as the crowd's loud protests.

The boy fainted, however, but the lashes continued.

Following the lashes, the boy was taken to a local hospital. His condition turned serious due to extreme pain and loss of blood. It took medical personnel a long time to revive the victim.

Lehi Central Command didn't appreciate the British behavior, and ordered the kidnapping of two British officers as promised. Two police personnel were taken to the same town, Nathanya, and to the same public square several hours later: one was a Major, the second was a Sergeant. With a crowd of hundreds gathering around to watch, the underground members removed their clothes to expose their backs just like the British did to the boy a short time before.

As soon as the authorities found out what's happening, British troops rushed to the area in a desperate attempt to stop the lashing of British subjects. However, they were stopped by a ring of fire from ambush. The troops, fired upon, were prevented from reaching the scene on time to prevent the execution on Lehi's retaliation.

Surprised and shocked at the "nerve" of Lehi fighters to punish British subjects, a first in the long British history, they seemed confused and at loss for words. No one in any part of the British Empire dared inflict similar punishment on British subjects, especially Police personnel. Meanwhile, the whip was used vigorously against their exposed bodies fifty times in succession. The crowds applauded following every moan and groan. Humiliated, British military and Police surrounded the town, enforcing strict curfew after the fact. Despite house to house searches, no underground members were found. No one was willing to testify and give details about underground activities either.

A second teenager, this time in Jerusalem, was caught pasting the underground wall-papers. He was arrested and tortured. The sixteen year old was pressed to reveal who told him to paste the papers. Witnesses stated that British detectives tortured the boy, beginning with pulling out the nails off his fingers, inflicting cigarette burns to his skin, as well as twisting his arms and legs. The boy didn't reveal anything. He didn't know who told him to paste the papers perhaps, or merely refused to talk. The British detectives, anxious to get results dunked his head in water until he couldn't breath. They covered the vulnerable parts of his body with wet towels and hit him, thus minimizing external signs of abuse.

The Police officer in-charge of the torture was Major James Farran. He was entrusted with the task of breaking the "terrorists" back and put a stop to their operations. He figured the young ones were easier to crack.

The torture continued for hours.

Due to the miscalculation of the boys medical condition, the teenager expired. Frantically trying to revive the boy, the major hoped the boy will survive. However, the wounds inflicted on the young body were too severe.

That's when Major Farran panicked.

He knew that if word got out that he resorted to such tactics, he would be signing his own death sentence. For that reason, no doubt, he took the boy's battered body and buried the remains in a field next to an Arab Village by the name of Abu-Gosh.

Apparently, Major Farran was certain that Arabs won't tell anybody what they have witnessed when it was done to a Jew. The major was unaware that this particular village of three hundred people, led by a Sheik named Abu-Gosh, was a member of Lehi along with his followers. They were committed to fight the British, perhaps reach an agreement with the Jewish people about their role in the new state. The first on Abu-Gosh's agenda was to get rid of British rule, and settle the Arab-Jewish disputes on their own later on.

The teenager's fate was reported to Central Command. Investigations revealed Major Farran to be responsible for the torture. An immediate order was issued to execute him for murder. Apparently, the major feared such a development, and with the consent of the authorities he was smuggled out of the country, doing the best they could to cover his trail.

It didn't take long for Central Command to locate Major Farran: he fled to London and hid in his brother's apartment. His brother, a priest, offered him refuge on Church property. It's unclear whether the priest knew the extent of his brother's involvement in the teenager's torture, and consequent murder.

Several days later, Lehi members in London located his hideout. Since it was Major Farran's birthday the week after, a letter was mailed to the Church addressed to Major James Farran.

The letter contained an explosive device, thin like a folded postcard, giving the impression that it was a greeting card.

The letter reached the Church on his birthday. Major Farran wasn't there. His brother, the priest, mistook the letter as his own and opened it. The explosion ripped his face apart, killing him instantly. As soon as the Major realized what happened to his brother, he fled, leaving the British Isles in a hurry.

Three weeks later, Major Farran was spotted in Toronto, Canada. Lehi members followed him but he managed to give them the slip. It took Lehi cells two weeks to spot the major again, this time in New York City. When Major Farran realized that Lehi members were on his trail, he tried to flee. However, this time his luck ran out: he was gunned down on Fifth Avenue, Manhattan. One direct hit to the heart was enough.

New York City police, unaware of the reason for his death, and since there were no clues, suspected it was a random killing, either criminal, or revenge, and left it at that.

CHAPTER EIGHT

The news about Etzel attacks on major British targets in Haifa spread fast throughout the country. Casualties were big among British forces due to the surprise element and very limited for Etzel itself. However, one Etzel member, 26 year old Dov Gronner, was severely wounded and captured.

His injuries included chest, head, legs and shoulder hits, which were difficult to treat. Since Gronner was the only one they captured alive, and believed they'd have a chance to interrogate, the British pressed a team of doctors to save his life, patch him up, and get him in condition for vigorous questioning.

Extensive medical patching followed involving hundreds of stitches. His body, shattered almost beyond repair, was put together as the saying goes "by spit and glue". The medics brought Gronner back to life, but he was barely living. British detectives worked on him day and night, yet were unable to get any useful information.

The way Etzel underground units were organized, it's doubtful whether he knew much unless he belonged to the top echelon. Even if Gronner knew anything beside his own activities, he didn't talk. The man, like all Lehi and Etzel members, were conditioned to keep their mouth shut, no matter what. For that reason the detectives wanted to use physical pressures to force him to talk.

The medical staff feared that if they tried anything vigorously physical they'll lose him altogether. Since their goal was to bring Gronner alive to trial, perhaps make an example out of him, they'd rather do anything possible to keep him alive.

The British Judge gave a short speech, and in his self-assured voice, swiftly pronounced sentence: **"You'll be hung by the neck until dead – God have mercy on your soul."**

As soon as the sentence turned public knowledge, Etzel declared that if the British hang Dov Gronner, they'll hang two British officers in retaliation. The British authorities, in their effort to minimize Etzel's threat, ignored it altogether. Etzel was true to its word: two British Sergeants were kidnapped and held in an unknown location pending execution should the British go ahead with Gronner's death sentence.

Massive searches, curfews and surprise raids followed, involving thousands of British troops and Police, yet the sergeants were not found. In the meantime the hanging of Dov Gronner proceeded according to plan. Since the man was very weak, unable to stand or walk, Police personnel held him up and carried his limp body to the rope for the hangman to tie the noose around his neck.

Usually when a human is hung, as soon as the neck is broken, the body reacts with violent tremors until death. Gronner, however, didn't move at all, and that led to speculation that he was already dead when they marched him to the gallows.

Shortly before the execution, Dov Gronner's sister, a U.S. citizen from New-York, rushed to the British Embassy and requested to pardon her brother since he was almost dead anyway.

The British authorities refused to consider the request.

Just as the sentence was carried out, and the press reported it in detail on the front pages, Etzel contacted the authorities to inform them that the sergeants will hang as scheduled. The British responded with threats to catch anyone involved and bring them all to justice. The British Justice, of course.

Following Etzel's declaration the families of the British sergeants appealed to underground leaders to have mercy on their families and spare their lives. It's not fair, they stated, to deprive the innocent children of their fathers.

The next day the British authorities were notified that the sergeants were executed as scheduled. The location of the hanging was in the forested area of Nathanya. As soon as British personnel located the sergeants surprise hit them: they realized that the dead bodies were cold and booby-trapped. Police personnel attempts to dismantle the wire tangles triggered an explosion, killing several high ranking officers. Police explosive experts as well as well as military were among the dead..

The British press published dozens of articles describing Etzel's barbaric execution as senseless, brutal and inhumane. Not one word, though, about the brutality of the British forces and their treatment of refugees, their handling of prisoners, and torture practices behind the scenes.

The British Police was always anxious to recruit natives to join their ranks. Since outgrowing the reporter job, being a Police officer seemed more appealing at that time, I applied hoping to become one. Readily accepted into the force, due to inspector Johnson's recommendation, my life changed drastically, going through the routine of daily discipline like: shining shoes, shaving, keeping a spotless uniform, and other rules and regulations prevalent during that period. If anyone failed inspection, he was summoned to the inspector in charge, asked to explain why he didn't perform as expected, and if the inspector didn't like the excuses the officer provided, he imposed two days stop-pay, sometimes more.

This meant a deduction of two days pay from the meager wages. There were times when native officers, both Arabs and Jews alike, suffering from disciplinary problems of that sort had very little money left at the end of the month in their pockets. Meaning they were barely able to pay their bills, feed themselves and their dependents.

Another drawback was that the British subjects and the natives had to follow different rules. For instance, a British officer carried a loaded gun with plenty ammunition, while a native wasn't permitted to carry a gun except in special cases, and even then, no bullets were provided.

The varied rules sounded more like discrimination, didn't it? Complaining to the inspector, or rather the "king", as we called him, was futile. The authorities didn't trust the natives, believing that restricting their ability to rebel would strengthen the British rule, if anyone considered the use of force against the authorities.

Since my abilities to read, write and speak English were recognized, my appointment as criminal investigator came next. The cases given to me were weird enough without having to understand Arabic, the language of most perpetrators. As a result someone who understood enough Arabic to translate was needed. Having several officers of Arab descent on staff was a plus since translators were readily available.

The reason for serving as a police officer was because my Lehi contact believed that my being part of the Palestinian Police Force could be beneficial to the underground. When the inspector as well as the sergeant heard about my knowledge of Hebrew and English, they quickly developed friendly relations with me. Thus, whenever they needed a written report, they entrusted me with the actual writing of the narratives in their names.

The sergeant, a chronic drunkard, couldn't even sign his name let alone write a report. The inspector, on the other hand, was a complete ignoramus, although his record showed that he had some education. He was a drunk as well but nobody deducted or stopped his pay for his damaging blunders as a result. They joined the Palestine Police when they responded to ads circulated in England encouraging British subjects to **"join the police and see the world."** They joined but they didn't see much of the world, anyway, because they had to devote most of their time to defend themselves against the undergrounds.

Due to the above they entrusted me with a very interesting investigation: the vehicular murder of an Arab pregnant young woman by a Polish soldier whose division was stationed in the south of the country. Apparently no one else wanted to take on the gruesome case, so they found me, young, naïve, untested with little knowledge of interrogation techniques except for the ability to write and speak English.

On arrival at the scene, and examining the sight, the body parts, including fetus tissues, I noted that they were spread all over the asphalt road. The job required listing bodily parts, their sizes, where exactly found, as well as the ages and names of the victim and witnesses.

Listing names was the easiest part. Listing ages was quite complicated: at that time the villagers had no birth certificates or any other means of certifying their date of birth. Determining birthdays required a series of questions like "when were you born?" The answer to that question would be something like that, "many years ago when the sun was up and the moon was down." It had some meaning, may be, in the original Arabic reply, but lost most of the meaning in the translation.

It took several hours to find out from witnesses and visual inspection of the premises that the victim crossed the road. She walked on the left side of the road when a military vehicle driven by the young Polish soldier veered left and hit her full force. The woman collapsed. She stumbled, falling straight down into the road at which time the driver corrected his turn, crushing and splashing body parts in The front wheels of the vehicle were covered with human strips of flesh. Both hands and legs, severed by the heavy hard wheels, decorated the asphalt with vivid red, just like in a classic painting. The driver didn't stop. He sped away, vanishing swiftly into the traffic ahead.

Arab witnesses stated that the woman was careful to stay on the left side of the road to avoid getting in the vehicle's way. The driver, turned deliberately, witnesses insisted, hit her from the back, and rolled over her body intentionally when she collapsed on the road. Since the vehicle left the scene, no one could ask the driver questions to verify witnesses accounts. Of course, digestion of my dinner became my biggest problem. Images of human flesh on the road floating in front of my eyes followed me, making it difficult to enjoy food.

Next case, two days later, was much more intriguing: an ax murder. It involved a newly married couple, an ax and a dead father of the bride. Several witnesses testified that a thirty seven year old man, a resident of Fradis village, offered the father of the bride one cow, one horse and a thousand Pounds for his fourteen year old daughter. The father agreed. However, the mother wasn't considered. The wedding was based on Muslim strict religious laws: some rituals as well as the beating of the bride severely on the first night to establish who is actually the "boss" in the new family unit.

The next day the fuming groom stormed into his in-laws home, demanding his property and money back from the bride's father. He claimed the fourteen year old daughter was not a virgin, and therefore, the agreement was void. The father was just as angry, denied the allegation, and refused to return or refund anything. Loud arguments, repeated accusations led to threats.

Neighbors verified the altercations.

The groom lifted an ax from the floor, which happened to be in the room, and in the heated war of words, he chopped the father's head in front of his wife and daughter. Their horrified screams alerted the neighbors to the scene. One of them notified the Police.

Since being assigned to the case, the squad car rushed to Fradis. On arrival, after examining the blood drenched scene, my questions centered whether or not the groom killed the man. The groom denied doing anything wrong.

"Neighbors informed me that you axed the man's head."

"I didn't kill the man."

"Your mother-in-law as well as your wife say you did."

"They are liars."

"There was no one else in the room - you think your mother in-law or your wife killed him?"

"I don't know," he said.

"Who did it, then?"

"I did not, must be Allah's will."

Allah's will revelation shocked me. "What does that mean?"

"I don't know."

"The ax didn't move by itself."

He insisted it wasn't him.

The officer who accompanied me snapped handcuffs on the groom's wrists at my request. The investigation confirmed that he murdered his father-in-law. Three weeks later he was brought before a Judge and sentenced to death by hanging. Four months thereafter he was executed. He insisted he was innocent of any wrong doing even when the hangman tightened the noose around his neck.

Cases like these kept me awake nights.

CHAPTER NINE

You may ask why I bring up investigations depicting the primitive ways of Arab villagers. This is to show what kind of people the Arabs were in those days. Facing such people was no problem by itself, but my suspicion was that the British used them to advance their agenda. The British tried to prolong their rule of the Land of Israel by any means possible. Their reluctance to leave was well known. These Arabs, obsessively religious, were easily influenced and swayed. That was perfect for the British way of "divide and conquer" policies.

The Arab economy was dependent on Jewish farmers who provided them with field jobs. They made a living mostly from growing, developing and selling agricultural products in Jewish towns and settlements. Since agriculture wasn't enough to support them financially, they sought work in Jewish towns as well as derived higher incomes by smuggling drugs. Being now a member of the Palestine Police I found out that smuggling of Hashish was a profitable occupation. From time to time officers were assigned to man random searches in order to curtail the drug business.

Due to a period of calm in criminal activity, like assaults, murders and thefts, many officers were kept busy fighting the surge in drug smuggling. Like many others, my assignment was to join one of those search parties. Several camels coming our way provided us with an interesting search for Hashish. We stopped the camel convoy in an open field and searched them one by one. Since the camel driver was calm, composed, and self-confident, we didn't suspect anything at all.

There was no evidence of criminal activity. We almost signaled the camel convoy to continue when my eyes spotted a few white threads sticking out from one of the camel's derrieres. Having no idea what it might be, and although "curiosity killed the cat" was a saying that proved correct most of the time, we took a chance and had a closer look.

"Hold it," I said, raising my hand.

The convoy stopped. The camel driver's face tightened a bit, while his eyes blinked excessively. At first my assumption was that dust irritated his eyes, but then there was no wind and no dust around.

We examined the white thread fibers close-up. When one of the officers pulled on it he declared, "There's something in there."

"Pull it out."

He pulled.

Out came a package draped in plastic wrapping. He kept on pulling and a second came out. When the packages came out the camel driver's face turned pale. He realized he was caught red handed.

"What is that?"

The camel driver stuttered, "I d-don't k-know."

Motioning officers on my right to detain the man created lots of excitement. While looking eight packages came out of the camel's body. Examining the substance in the packages, we determined that it was either Hashish or Opium. Each camel had a similar collection of drugs. The catch was the biggest find in the area despite many other precincts downplaying the find to claim credit for it later on for themselves.

The camel driver was arrested, his camels confiscated, and all drugs were held for evidence. He was booked for smuggling. Whatever happened to the drugs, and the driver, we had no idea since they were transferred to another jurisdiction for handling.

About that time Central Command informed the cell under my control to be alert and listen to anything that might develop. The news was depressing: intelligence reached Central Command that British Police personnel were temporarily assigned to fight refugee landings. However, no one knew anything of the coming attack on police headquarters in Haifa. I knew that records of suspected Lehi members were kept there under lock and key on that location.

Lehi was always short of funds. In order to buy explosives in the international black market, the underground movement needed more money than they could collect from donations. For that reason they entrusted Yaaqov Garnek, a Lehi operations officer, to provide the needed money for most underground activities. The man, known publicly by the nickname, "the tall blond," organized the biggest robbery of Barclays Bank Tel-Aviv branch the first time in the history of that financial institution.

Intelligence reports provided details about a big bank deposit in that branch. Shortly after the money, about fifty million Pounds, was deposited, several blocks around the bank were sealed, covered and secured by Lehi members just in case British forces will rush to the rescue. "The tall blond" and several of his men dressed in British military uniforms arrived at the bank with big bags to collect money due for British troops payroll.

They had proper credentials, looked exactly like legitimate typical Englishmen and spoke, for the most part, English with a British accent. Having no problems with identity, they stuffed the bags with all the money they could find. The bags contained bills of one Pound, five Pounds, ten Pounds, Twenty and a Hundred. "The tall blond" thanked the bank manager for his cooperation, signed for it and they all walked out from the bank as fast as they came in.

The vehicle waiting for them was swiftly loaded with money bags. To make their escape easier, they decided to leave behind one of the bags in order to have enough room for the others. They believed the bag contained one Pound bills. "The tall blond" and his men were picked up by other vehicles waiting around the corner.

Within ten minutes, the area was cleared.

Traffic resumed as soon as the jams unscrambled. The public had no idea what's happening until bank security personnel noticed one money bag left behind. They called the military to inform them that one big bag was left behind. As soon as it became clear that the military didn't pick up the money, they realized it was a robbery.

The police was immediately alerted.

The bag left behind was opened: it contained one Hundred Pound bills, rather than the one Pound bills "the tall blond" and his men assumed. The robbery, although successful, due to the blunder, didn't net as much as they hoped.

Investigations led to detention of people for identification purposes. The intense questioning produced more questions than answers. As a last resort, the authorities imposed curfews on a vast area which translated into meticulous searches. Yet, the intense efforts brought no results. They found no trace of imposter British soldiers, their vehicles or the money bags taken.

However, as far as Lehi finances were concerned, the money taken from Barclays Bank arrived too late to be used for the coming operation in Haifa police headquarters. Having no funds to buy the proper explosives, underground chemists and engineers created explosive materials from orange and grapefruit crusts. They used wooden barrels stuffed with these crude explosives. Instead of using dynamite they used the substitutes which proved to be a lot less efficient, but quite effective for the purpose needed. The barrels, when rolled to hit the target, smashed hard against the building housing police headquarters. The room, where detailed files about underground members were located, burst into flames, consuming all paper records.

The mission, as far as Lehi was concerned, was a success.

The British lost all accumulated intelligence details supplied by Mapai and Mapam zealots (in Hebrew: <u>Miflegett Hapoalim & Miglegethh Poalim Meuhedeth)</u>, which constituted labor led by David Ben-Gurion. Ben-Gurion hoped it would help the British arrest or kill all citizens either members or supporters of Lehi and Etzel. David Ben-Gurion, who most of the world believed was an angel, did his best to eliminate his opposition. If you were against him he treated you like an enemy. If you didn't agree with him, you were doomed.

The operation lasted no longer than fifteen to twenty minutes. The British forces within the building, taken by surprise, didn't know the explosion and flames were result of an attack. When they realized it was too late to identify the personnel involved.

CHAPTER TEN

Many Jewish youths arrested on suspicion of belonging to a terror organization, namely Lehi and Etzel, were detained and incarcerated in Acre prison. In effect, neither Lehi nor Etzel were actually terror organizations by definition. They didn't target civilians, and in particular children, women or babies like Hamas, Hizballah, Jihadists, and the rest of them do nowadays.

Acre prison inmate numbers reached several hundred, despite the fact that not all agreed with the undergrounds way of fighting. Desperate to impose their will on the Jewish population, the British propaganda referred to members of Lehi, Etzel including anyone who expressed opposition to the British rule, as murderers and criminals.

In a symbolic operation for freedom, Lehi's special forces attacked prison authorities from two directions simultaneously: Lehi members pushed in from the outside, incarcerated-members pushed the guards from the inside. Hundreds of prisoners took advantage of the opportunity and fled without a trace, among them charged with minor as well as major infractions including Arabs who fit that description.

Following the prison break, the British imposed laws against carrying any type of arms, or ammunition. All buses, coming or leaving Haifa were searched. In particular, men of any age that had a moustache went through a grueling interrogation. Sometimes they were detained for further questioning just because they looked suspicious even though they had proper ID, alibis and spoke Hebrew only.

As it happened, I boarded a bus to visit my sister in Kiriyat-Motzkin, a suburb of Haifa. The standing orders from Central Command for Lehi members at that time were clear: we must carry weapons to avoid being caught alive, thus perhaps endanger the lives of other members. If Police officers arrested anyone for being a member in the underground, his duty was to do everything possible to escape, including killing himself as a last resort. That was designed to prevent British Intelligence from finding out who's associated with Central Command.

Following the standing instructions my pocket had a hand-grenade tucked in plus a small caliber pistol loaded and ready to fire. Police officers stopped the bus for a meticulous search in the vicinity of Atlith. One police officer entered the bus, a second officer walked behind him, his trigger-finger ready.

If the police officer found my hand-grenade, the pistol or even a bullet, it was my duty to kill him and try to escape. If I failed to do so I'd be a sitting duck. Should the British find anything illegal in my possession, I'd be automatically sentenced to death by hanging. Looking around it was clearly impossible to escape since a big number of police officers surrounded the bus during the search. These officers were equipped with high power weapons as well as automatic pistols.

Unable to reveal my being in the Palestine Police as an accredited criminal investigator since that would oblige me to offer a convincing reason and clarify my presence in civilian clothes, plus the reason for carrying a grenade and a pistol which were not provided by the police department to natives.

Taking a chance divulging my being a police officer or being caught red handed as a civilian was crucial for my survival. Before I could make up my mind what to do next, the police officer was next to me. Pretending not to notice him, my attention focused on anything but him.

The current Palestine Post Daily issue was spread in front of me. Pretending being so engrossed reading front-page news that I couldn't see the officer approaching. He touched my shoulder to get my attention, and asked, "Do you speak English?" Apparently the Daily Paper in my possession gave me away.

Lifting my eyes slowly, exhibiting surprise to see the officer towering over me, I asked, "Excuse me, officer – are you talking to me?"

"Yes, sir."

"What was the question, please?"

He smiled pleasantly when he realized my English diction and fluency. "The question was if you speak English, sir."

"Oh yes, officer, I do. I have a degree from a British College."

"I see," he looked me over. "Any good news in the paper, sir?"

Trying to sound friendly, my assumption was that he attempted to soften me up. "Not really - the usual crime reports."

Both officers seemed pleased with my English vocabulary. It felt like taking an English exam all over again. The first officer looked around, and said, "Sorry to disturb you, sir."

"You're not disturbing me – why all this, officer – did anything happen today?"

"You didn't hear?"

"Hear – what, officer?"

"Terrorists took over Acre prison and released hundreds of criminals and dangerous terrorists."

Pretending displeasure, my voice raised by an octave or two, "There's nothing about it in the paper, officer."

"It happened a short time ago. It'll probably be in the evening editions."

The friendly conversation apparently paid off.

He touched my shoulder again, warning me to be careful, since I may be sitting next to a dangerous terrorist and never know it. Promising to be very careful, of course, it seemed to satisfy him. Being proficient in English contributed to his trust. He didn't search me, nor did he frisk any part of my clothing. Why he didn't I'd never know. In his place I'd have. It's possible he simply forgot, I have an innocent face or maybe he didn't believe that anyone with a British Diploma could indeed be a member of a "dangerous" underground organization against British rule.

Other passengers were not so lucky. The officers detained some of them, questioned others in detail, especially when they had a moustache above the upper lip and mediocre knowledge of the English language.

While police officers interrogated the passengers my eyes continued to scan news reports. My interest centered on Anshel Spilman, a Lehi member, one of the original twenty one escapees from Latroon detention camp. My eyes, scanning the entire front page almost line by line, caught the mention of the trial, now just beginning. Anshel Spilman was caught in a search-sweep with a pistol and ammunition before he had a chance to use any of it as the standard instructions required him to do.

Digging into his past, detectives discovered that he was one of the twenty one original escapees. That revelation encouraged the Prosecutor to add to the charge of carrying a deadly weapon with ammunition, that he was an active member of stature in a terrorist organization, namely, The Stern Gang, as the British Governor called it. Carrying a deadly weapon was bad enough. It was considered a criminal offense punishable by death. The British enjoyed netting one of the original "big fish", intending to squeeze as much propaganda scores as possible.

Being a "big fish" in a dangerous terrorist organization was an achievement. Since that was a death penalty offense as well, and he couldn't be executed twice, I wondered what punishment could they impose – torture, maybe? The British, per their official sources, never tortured anyone. We all knew the contrary, and some Lehi members experienced their expertise in that area many times. Many torture cases in the coming pages will be coming alive soon, and described in detail. They are definite proof of their existence.

The trial lasted several days. Among other questions the accused was required to respond to, he was asked if he had an attorney, otherwise the Court will appoint one to defend him free of charge. That, the British believed, will prove to the world how nice and fair British Courts were. When permitted to speak, Anshel Spilman declined a Court appointed attorney. He expressed his thanks, but stated he'd rather defend himself.

Following the Prosecutor's presentation of his "crimes" the Judge asked if he had anything to say to his defense, Anshel Spilman replied, yes indeed, he had a lot to say. The judge didn't know what he was getting into: Spilman spoke for about five hours, explaining to the Court and the world, should anyone care to listen, that it's definitely not a crime to fight against the enemies of your people who occupy your homeland, the land called Eretz Israel (The Land of Israel), and not Palestine, as the British called it, being an enemy from the start despite their useless pledges of support.

The opening statement hit the Court like a rocket. The judge, assuming a bored look, looked hurt when he heard the first sentence. Anshel Spilman raised his voice and said, "Who are you to judge me for fighting for my people's freedom in our homeland?" He paused, looked into the judge's eyes, and went on, **"Please remember the historical fact that when my people were a civilized nation, giving the world the Bible and the Ten Commandments, yours were still hopping from tree to tree!"**

The judge's face soured instantly, his eyes centered on the defendant like a laser beam. He tried to impress that the British Justice System was fair, and to strengthen that impression he didn't interrupt or stop him for five long hours.

When the defendant completed his defense speech, the silence in the courtroom was so thick one could feel the pressure in the air. Whether the people agreed or disagreed with the factual fabric of the speech they didn't show it.

The judge cleared his throat while the prosecutor raised his voice. He asked to find the defendant guilty and demanded the death penalty. Following the prosecutor's demand the crowd in the courtroom burst into loud arguments some for and many against.

Requesting silence in the court that all present seemed to ignore, the judge used his gavel several times in succession to reestablish calm. Each time he banged the gavel it sounded louder than before, indicating how upset he was for losing control of the situation.

Rather agitated, his glowing blue eyes shifting nervously around, he stated, "This court listened patiently to your defense speech and finds you guilty as charged. It is the opinion of this Court that your guilt was proven without the shadow of a doubt. Your crimes are punishable by death: you'll hang by the neck until dead. God have mercy on your soul."

Expecting the verdict, Spilman didn't react.

Many attending the Court's procedure found it difficult to believe that the accused was a terrorist in the first place. Some said he didn't impress them as a violent man. Others maintained that it had something to do with the saying that "still waters run deep."

The scheduled execution was supposed to take place within four to six weeks. However, the execution had to be canceled: two weeks later Anshel Spilman was freed from jail by a daring Lehi operation which caught the jailers by surprise.

The press gave different accounts of the operation: some maintained that Lehi members infiltrated the jailing crowd and when attacked from the outside, the members inside took over the jail so fast that the warden had no time to consider the consequences. Other sources revealed that a number of jail personnel were actually Lehi members who overpowered the warden and forced him to release the prisoner.

Whatever version was correct it's impossible to tell since both made sense and headlines. The result: Spilman was allowed to escape without a trace and no one had a clue where to find him.

CHAPTER ELEVEN

The British major weapon was used again: immediate and strict curfews on cities entailing a sweep of vast areas in the hope that a quick reaction would net either Spilman or anyone who participated in his escape. The tension between the undergrounds and the authorities intensified. British frustrations increased to the extent of carelessness, so did anxieties and anger within the local population.

Despite the overwhelming speed the British failed to find anyone connected to Spilman's release either in Jerusalem, Tel-Aviv or Haifa. However, the Tel-Aviv sweep involved the killing of five toddlers, three or four years old, playing with toy vehicles on balconies. Children always played on balconies with plastic vehicles, making humming noises to imitate roaring engines. The nervous soldiers, frozen by fear, reacted to any noise with rapid fire. Fear can cause panic, sure, but engine roaring and children's voices differ. Whether the soldiers fired because they wanted to cause damage, thus scare off an attack, or knew that killing some civilians or children didn't warrant punishment.

Were the soldiers Anti-Semitic characters for shooting Jewish children because they felt they could do it with no fear of punishment or they were afraid of shadows and unexplained noise? They were nervous, sure, fearing attacks any minute that would jeopardize their lives, but shooting children was a little too much.

Many British soldiers were Arab sympathizers, however, not all British soldiers were Anti-Semitic. Many were even sympathizers of the Zionist aspirations as a result of the holocaust. That, however, didn't change the fact, that the government they served, especially Ernst Bevan, the Foreign Secretary, didn't give a damn about anyone but his own selfish needs, the British crown and British interests.

Being familiar with the incident enabled me write a strongly worded article in the underground's wall paper. I expressed anger against having laws on the books allowing troops to shoot children at will. Yet, no one called the British soldiers terrorists. When Lehi attacked a police or military stronghold and a civilian was killed, like the spouse of an officer or the child of one, the entire world was informed, up in arms, and the undergrounds were called cold blooded "murderers", "blood thirst killers" etc. Now, that the troops killed Jewish children, no one called them names.

The press, local as well as British, tried to justify the careless reaction due to nerves and psychological pressures. No one was on the side of the children, and many even blamed the parents for allowing them to play on balconies.

Among other incidents, not publicly known, was the case of a seventeen year old girl in Jerusalem arrested on suspicion of being a member of Lehi. Once again, British detectives pressed her to reveal names of members that in effect, she couldn't know or wouldn't reveal.

While in detention in Jerusalem, one of the detectives threatened the girl that if she didn't cooperate he'll bring trained dogs to rape her. Whether they had such trained dogs was unclear. Later on, the same detective, anxious to excel in his job, threatened her to have big men from Africa abuse her sexually. The term "big men from Africa" scared that young girl to death, in particular, probably because she was short, skinny and physically weak.

The woman in the next cell, an Arab arrested for stealing, heard parts of the interrogation, including the threats. That woman had many visitors, and being upset, she confided in her father and told him what she heard. The father, told his neighbors. The neighbors told others until finally it reached the ears of a Lehi member who was a resident of Abu-Gosh village.

It wasn't known whether anyone was authorized to threaten the girl that way or the detective decided to use the tactic on his own. When the report reached Central Command it was decided to handle it with no delay. The next day the detective found a note on his desk in English. The note advised him that Lehi knew of his interrogating methods and should any harm come to the girl or any other girl whether member of the underground or not, they'll hold him personally responsible and punish him accordingly. Furthermore, the note indicated that Central Command knew he had a family, a wife and a seven year old daughter. They informed him that they knew where he lived and where he spent leisure time with his family. Should he implement any of his threats, the same fate will await them.

Shortly thereafter the seventeen year old girl was promptly released. The detective involved was no longer seen anywhere, and it's possible he was encouraged to flee the country, thus blend into another jurisdiction. Someone should have reminded the detective what happened to Major Farran. The man believed he could escape punishment by running away.

He didn't make it either.

The British behavior contributed to a Polish Brigade soldier stationed in the country to threaten and insult a passer by. This soldier, encouraged by British hostile attitudes toward the local population, namely, the natives, either Arabs or Jews, attacked this Jewish man whose beard he thought belonged to a Rabbi. It so happened that this young man was indeed an orthodox rabbi. Forcibly, the Polish soldier threatened to cut his throat if he resisted. He shaved the rabbi's beard with an obvious intention to insult the man and show how much he disrespected the Jewish religion. In another case, a Polish soldier ran over with a truck a pregnant young woman and killed her and her fetus. Witnesses stated he did it on purpose. This one, however, escaped and was never heard of again.

As expected, when Lehi's Central Command was notified of the incident the Polish soldier was fingered by the rabbi. Two Lehi members swiftly reacted before he had time to object. The members shoved him into a vehicle and took him to an empty apartment in Tel-Aviv. While the man didn't speak Hebrew, he understood basic English as well as a few curses in Arabic.

He was informed that he was on trial by Lehi for shaving the rabbi's beard. For this, he was told, he was judged and sentenced. Not revealing immediately what the sentence implied, the soldier's fuse shortened, He raised his voice and asked, ""So, what you going to do?"

"We are going to shave you."

The soldier smiled, "Oh, that, I didn't mean nothing by it, just a joke, you know."

"Maybe in Poland it's a joke, here it's equivalent to murder."

His face tightened, "I don't hate Jews," he said, his voice shaky. "I respect all religions. But, if it'll make you happy, go ahead, shave me."

Both Lehi members burst into loud laughter. "You agree to be shaved?"

"Yes, sure - why not?"

"Okay then, take your pants off."

"What – what does that mean?"

"I'm a doctor," one of the boys said. "I'll shave your manly pride and make you a perfect female, how d'you like that?"

"No, please, don't do that, I really…"

"Yes, I know, you love Jews."

When the boys unzipped his pants and pulled them down, he covered his genitals with his trembling hands. "You can't do that, really, it's illegal!"

"Did you ask the rabbi permission to shave him?"

The soldier didn't answer, instead he concentrated on the knife in one of the boys hand. "Don't, please don't!"

"Give me a good reason not to do it."

"It's not fair!"

The boy pretending to be a doctor said, "Hold him tight, Yoni, let's get it over with."

"If he screams people may try to stop us, don't you think?"

"If he screams shove this handkerchief down his throat. Here, use this one!"

Next came a scream, the rolling of the eyes and a muffled moan as he collapsed on the hard floor. That's when the operation stopped. They had no intention of going through with it, anyway, but since that moment, no Polish soldier tried anything similar. As a matter of fact, no one else, British or otherwise, tried either.

CHAPTER TWELVE

Rumors spread among the Jewish masses dealt with stories about Arab atrocities against a Jewish settlement in the Negev. It was believed that Arabs attacked and conquered the settlement while all men of military age were in the frontlines. Women, children, babies, and the elderly were the only ones there.

It wasn't publicized when Arab militants took over the settlement, slaughtered everyone in sight, including pets and livestock. They crushed chicken eggs, killed cows, donkeys, cats and dogs. The **Allah Akbar** battle cry dominated the gruesome scene of blood and body parts. The reason given by Arab sources was that they had to be destroyed because they were Jewish. The Koran, militants believed, ordered them to kill infidels, especially Jews.

These rumors made some underground members jittery. When Lehi moved to secure vital strategic parts of Jerusalem, they came across an Arab village called Dir Yassin. As they took positions to prevent Moslem extremists to advance into Jewish neighborhoods, a hail of bullets met them. Naturally, they returned fire. The extremists were forced to retreat but the battle continued. During the battle most villagers were killed. The extremists, as always, were hiding among civilians, seeking refuge from bullets aimed at them in medical facilities and schools. The civilian extremists used as shields were all killed, including a big number of their own men.

That was the only version the public heard about, and immediately the battle became political football. Sympathizers of Lehi and Etzel repeated the undergrounds' reports, while the parties leaning to the left, who used it as a political tool, blamed the undergrounds for killing civilians. The left's contention of a massacre aided and abetted the extensive Moslem propaganda machine, which was always more effective than their fighting dexterity.

Jew haters as well as Anti-Semites all over the world caught on to it and used Dir Yassin as a good reason to smear Zionism. Media, in many countries, maintained that Jewish refugees that escaped Nazi atrocities were doing to the Muslims exactly what the Germans did to them. Until this very day, Neo-Nazis and Leftists are united against anything Israel is doing in self defense.

However, during that period, friction between what the labor movement labeled "rightists" or "nationalists" and members of the undergrounds, namely, Etzel, Lehi and the Heruth party, believed the latter version. The frictions led to propaganda wars. The labor movements labeled underground members names like Fascists, and the undergrounds labeled the labor movement Communists and stupid Socialist extremists.

That's the time when the labor movement began a whisper offensive calling any of the undergrounds operations, including their supporters, "un-educated" and stupid. There was no state yet, but the power struggle was at full swing.

The hatred, intimidation and name calling between the different trains of thought increased ten fold. It should be mentioned that even at that time within a population of about half a million, the Jews had thirty seven political parties competing with each other for power. Whenever anyone said anything they didn't appreciate they called him or her "un-educated", namely: ignorant, stupid or Fascist.

That led to a massive verbal attack against Menachem Begin who represented the nationalist movement. The friction, many a time, came to fist fights, loud curses, and insults. Many labor leaders claimed that Begin's party consisted mostly of religious extremists, Jews of Spanish ancestry and uneducated individuals. That was meant to imply that supporters of Begin were other than European descendants, namely, violent non-progressive people. In other words, they considered anyone not in agreement with them as low life and ignorant.

Contrary to general propaganda belief, there were plenty of European descendants in the undergrounds. Despite the fact that laborites enjoyed calling themselves enlightened progressives, I didn't meet many bright and considerate ones among them. They were arrogant and obnoxious, and highly opinionated just like the Russian Communists who blamed the whole world for global problems, except themselves.

David Ben-Gurion, the labor chief, whose reputation was advanced internationally as a statesman of stature, was one of them. As long as you applauded him and said "yes" to whatever he aspired, you were a patriot. If you disagreed, you're ignorant and low life.

The left under the leadership of Mapai (in Hebrew United Workers Party) encouraged teasing and violence so that many youths believed that standing and smoking cigarettes in front a synagogue on Friday night, being an irritant to religious people, was patriotic. Nationalists, however, couldn't tolerate religious intolerance and dispatched their youths to resist such disrespect. Fist fights developed causing bitterness throughout the country, dividing the people further. The saying that Jews are united was always a farce: if they were united as some people believe, they wouldn't have lost their independence twice in history: first against the Greeks, second against the Romans.

The Hebrews, Judeans, the Jews and Israelis, all names implying ancient Israel, were known to have many opinions, When they got together their opinions were vastly different. That's where the joke originates in the saying that when "two Jews get together they have three opinions."

CHAPTER THIRTEEN

British forces continued to mistreat refugees. Their crime was seeking life in their historical homeland. Lehi and Etzel undergrounds accelerated their attacks to slow them down. The three underground movements, Lehi, Etzel and the Hagana (ruled and directed by labor) reached an agreement to fight British policies together. This was the first time since their founding, all three movements united against the British. No matter what carrots the British offered labor, similar successful systems of **divide and conquer** policies elsewhere, failed this time to work in Eretz Israel (The Land of Israel).

On the same day, at the same time, all British military and police installations, including airports, were attacked to prevent them from fighting refugees arriving in big numbers, mostly direct escapees from well-known Nazi concentration camps. Since the British forces were kept busy, the refugees landed with little opposition. They exchanged clothing with locals and were given Identification Cards. They were provided jobs as well as dwellings.

British anger reached new highs. They imposed curfews everywhere, detaining thousands of people in massive sweeps in an attempt to catch the so-called "terrorists", either crush or kill them on the spot.

The tense situation turned dangerous. The confrontations increased, poisoning many minds. Clashes killed and maimed people on both sides. The tension lasted a long time until finally United Nations Security Council decided to step in. By a majority of votes, the UN imposed a partition of the Land of Israel, in which most of the land was allocated to the Arabs for a Palestinian state and only a tiny part allocated for a Jewish state.

Jordan which was awarded by the British half of what was known as ancient Israel. The eastern half of the land was allocated to be for two states: thirty percent was declared an Arab state and twenty percent for the Jewish state. If you add up the division of the land you'll come up with eighty percent for the Arabs (Jordan, the West Bank and Gaza Strip) and only twenty percent for the Jews. In effect, four fifths of the Land of Israel was given to the

Arabs, while only one fifth of the original Land of Israel was allocated to Israel. If this is justice by any definition, I wonder what injustice would be!

In May 1947 the Jewish population under the rule of the leftist labor movement with David Ben-Gurion in a leadership position, was forced by Lehi and Etzel operations to declare the establishment of Israel as a Democratic independent state. The Arabs, rejected the partition altogether. They wanted all the territory to be a Palestinian state with no provision for Jews, period.

However, President Harry Truman of United States, was the first to recognize the State of Israel, thus creating a lead for others to follow. As a goodwill gesture, before the implementation of UN resolution to leave the mandated country, the British accelerated confiscation of all guns and ammunition in Jewish communities. The idea was that the Arabs will attack and massacre enough Jews thus their supporters will raise hell, especially U.S. Jews, including others of the same political interests, demanding to put a stop to it. As a result, the British hoped they'll be urged to return in order to restore the rule of law. Of course, they'd be happy to play judge and jury once again.

Encouraged by British declarations as well as pro-Arab behavior on the ground, thirteen Arab states in the Middle East declared war against the State of Israel. Their generals promised the Palestinians that they'll conquer the land, throw the Jews into the sea, take over their properties, livestock, including their women, and anything else of value. The spoils of war, the Arabs believed, will be given to the local Arabs. Thus they'll establish their state over the Land of Israel. Once facts will be established on the ground the UN partition decision will be null and void.

As a result, the Palestinians were urged by the Arab states to leave the land temporarily. They'll be allowed to return, inherit anything of value in the land, including livestock and women. The Palestinians were very anxious to leave, confident that the Arab states will succeed. After all, considering the numerical odds, Israel had no chance.

Faced with such a reality, all three undergrounds joined the Israeli Defense Forces in a hurry. The infant Israeli army appointed me recruiter in charge of deciding who will join the army in Zikhron-Yaaqov area, and when they should report for duty. Recruiting had to be based on age, with some exceptions, depending on family size and hardships, if any.

That's when problems popped up: my parents' neighbors attempted to influence my mother to convince me to excuse their children from military service. Human nature was human nature: they supported whole heartedly the fight for freedom and independence, but were willing to let others do the fighting for them.

Consequently, many of them wouldn't talk to my parents when they found out that I refused to be intimidated. My job, as a recruiter, was to excuse a son if his family had no other children of military age. The idea was to excuse any family's children due to hardships, and supply them with a white ID card confirming the deferment. Families with two children or more, only one would have to join immediately. Other families, with more children, would get a red card each, meaning they'll be required to report for duty right away.

Following implementation of these rules, my mother had no friends and none of her neighbors would talk to her. They told her that I, the recruiter, was sending their children to the frontlines to die while I stayed behind, away from harm's way.

Even the most vocal patriots behaved that way.

They agreed that someone has to fight the enemy, sure, but their children should be excused. When a family of four had two of their sons ordered to report for duty, and actually participated in battle, that's when my biggest problem surfaced: both of them came back missing limbs, one lost a leg, the other lost both legs. People with sons in the military, because of my recruiting activities, labeled me coward. They maintained I was sending others to die but I was hiding, supposedly, under the bed. As soon as wounded came back in bigger numbers, they added to the original label of coward and declared me murderer and a blood thirsty idiot.

Realizing that this could not continue that way for long without affecting my mental health, I contacted the military and requested to join the active service. The first two requests were ignored. After repeating the request several more times the military gave up, allowing me to join. Someone else, from a neighboring town, was appointed recruiter instead.

Like all other Lehi members, I was assigned to the Eight Commando Brigade equivalent to the Special Forces in the USA. That Brigade consisted of Etzel, Lehi and Palmach, (the Special Forces associated with labor). It so happened, that Major Moshe Dayan was organizing his special unit, designated as the 89th regiment. General Itzchak Sadeh was in charge of the Southern Command, thus in-charge of their planning and operational moves. Itzhak Rabin, was the Colonel in-charge of the brigade.

Moshe Dayan chose officers from a prepared list of veterans from all three movements. They were selected to be speed-trained and serve in the regiment he was entrusted to command.

The new recruits, including myself, were told to form several lines. Finding myself in the first line, I doubted it made any difference since he had information about all of us, including experience, education and assessed capabilities from which to decide his preferences.

Major Dayan looked at his list with his one seeing eye, examined each recruit, evaluated his impressions and decided on several dozen individuals who would become officers in his regiment, after they'd pass all requirements essential for the rank: being educated, having leadership ability, be physically and mentally healthy. The most important was the ability to make right and quick decisions under fire. Moshe Dayan believed that hesitation in battle could cost lives.

Before anyone could figure out what to do next, the vigorous training period started. Most recruits chosen to be commissioned and non-commissioned officers were skilful in use of weapons, strategies, and communications. How to advance or retreat, if necessary, came next. The final test was to lead a platoon in actual battle, attack and capture positions behind enemy lines.

Only individuals who succeeded with minimum casualties were designated to become combat officers. Individuals indicating adaptability but failed to lead would become Sergeants subject to numerous minor additional tests.

Within several weeks, after capturing an enemy position by sneaking under cover of darkness, taking them by surprise, Major Dayan entrusted me to command a platoon, and later on a company as well. The members of my platoon were all "generals" in their own mind, of course, and each one advised me or anyone who would listen, how to plan attacks, what strategy to follow etc. To command a unit full of "generals" wasn't an easy feat: they all thought they knew it all without even knowing basics. You probably met many people in every walk of life that knew better than anyone else without even trying.

The first order of the day, as soon as I took command of the company, was to form a disciplined lineup and listened to what I had to say. "As of now I'm your commanding officer," was my first order of the day. "You address me either by rank or Commander. If you want to complain, you must present your complaint to your Corporal, he will present it to your Sergeant, and only the Sergeant will present it to the Second Lieutenant, the Second Lieutenant will present it to me, your commanding officer. Is that understood?"

The expression on many faces indicated boredom. Some cracked knuckles, exchanging words of a rebellious nature between them. The complaints were loud enough to reach my ears. What I heard wasn't pleasant, it was a string of curses and abusive language. Unable to tolerate abusive language forced me to order Sergeant Benjamin to have the platoon stand at attention.

The Sergeant's voice was so loud even the deaf could hear him. "The platoon will now stand at attention – a t t e n t i o n!"

Many soldiers smiled, some laughed, the others were in no rush to obey. The biggest drawback was lack of discipline. Military, that is. During the undergrounds period they all obeyed blindly, no questions asked.

"Very well," I said. "You had your fun, now listen and listen good." They were not attentive. "We can get along only if you respond positively to basic requirements: first - obey your COs without question. Disobey and you'll be punished. Second: don't use abusive language in my presence. Should abusive language reach my ears despite my request, that individual will have his mouth washed with soap in public."

Most of them doubted the warning: they smiled and moved aimlessly around. Some giggled. One individual raised his hand and before anyone could ask him anything, he yelled aloud, "Sorry, Commander, you have no right to wash anyone's mouth with soap without a court martial!"

The laughter was ear shuttering.

"Very well, then," my voice was loud for all to hear. "You want proof that it'll be done - here it is – you, third in line, come here!"

"What for –and why me?"

"I heard you use abusive language."

"Yes," he said, "so what – all of us use it - this is the army, man!"

Sergeant Benjamin forced and dragged the soldier to face me. "What's your name, private?"

"Elie," he smiled.

I whispered into the Sergeant's ear, "Go get the soap from the kitchen."

"No need, Commander, I have some in my tent."

Elie giggled as Sergeant Benjamin left. "What now?" he asked.

"I have a surprise for you, private Elie."

"Yes, Commander, I love surprises – how did you know that?"

Sergeant Benjamin was back, handing me a bottle of water and a bar of soap. "Hold him steady, Sergeant."

"Yes, Commander," he said and grabbed Elie before he could think or move. As long as Elie fought Sergeant Benjamin it was impossible to restrain him long enough.

In order to expedite things I asked , "Any volunteers?"

My request for assistance brought a few dozen forward.

"Hold it, I need only two, no more."

"The first two to respond, come over here," the sergeant said. "All others move back to your positions."

The two chosen to help Sergeant Benjamin were big and muscular. They had no trouble restraining Elie at first try. I splashed water on Elie's face and mouth, rubbed soap on his lips, spreading suds generously all over him. He cursed as the Sergeant forced his mouth open. I rubbed soap into his mouth and tongue making certain soap covered his mouth in and out.

Elie tried to free himself but Sergeant Benjamin and the volunteers held him so tight he could hardly move. Elie wasn't strong and fast enough to escape. Having soap in his mouth wasn't very pleasant either, he found out as he spat in all directions to clear the soapy taste. The recruits in line watched the procedure with intense interest. No one laughed this time. Elie stopped his cursing habit. He was too busy spitting soap suds.

"Give me some water," he begged. "I'm choking, sir!"

"Choking, sir? I'm your Commander, Elie, remember?"

"Yes, sir, Commander…water…please!"

As I gave him the bottle, the soldiers in line laughed hysterically. Elie rinsed his mouth, spitting soap in all directions. No matter how many times he spat soap, when he tried to say something the soap turned into a series of successive bubble bursts.

Later I found out from his friends that he spat bubbles for two long days. Since that day no one in the unit cursed, used abusive language or criticized my rules. Not in my presence. Not that I could hear anyway. However, some of them labeled me crazy, but none used abusive language or curses as freely as before.

CHAPTER FOURTEEN

Facing the Arab Legion, the best of Arab armies, known as Jordanian troops trained and led by British officers, was a big challenge. My unit had only one Stan sub-machine-gun that fired intermittently, limited ammunition, and a number of attack hand-grenades. Attack hand-grenades and defense hand-grenades differed: attack grenades produced lots of noise and caused little damage while defense grenades caused lots of damage producing minimal noise.

Information floating around indicated that the Legion intended to move on Tel-Aviv, the most populated city within reach. As a result, my unit rushed to dig into the rocky terrain entrusted with the task of stopping the Legionnaires should they try to break through.

Dig in as fast as possible was the direct order from Major Dayan, followed by a slogan that became well known over the years: **"sweat saves blood!"** Many soldiers, facing such a well equipped enemy for the first time in their lives, didn't dig deep enough. When the Jordanian Legion began their fierce artillery bombardments, we suffered very heavy casualties.

This was a very effective lesson.

The digging intensified to the point that could offer shelter from direct hits, especially if it was dug in zigzag shape. Half of my unit was either dead or maimed. New recruits reached my unit as replacements, this time mostly from foreign volunteer sources that hardly spoke the language.

Now, giving a command in Hebrew became a problem. Besides training to face the enemy the company had to solve the language problem fast. Basic commands were taught in a hurry, but the confusion was more than I could take. When gunners were ordered to aim left, they aimed right, and vice versa.

Should the situation continue, we may all get killed.

Many foreign recruits claimed to be experts in military affairs due to their service as commanders in foreign armies. I had doubts about that, since their solutions didn't follow military logic. Although conditions were vastly different, they expressed opposing views, criticizing every step on the way, doubting strategies mostly of a hit and run nature under darkness cover. They obeyed orders reluctantly, and for a while, only following threats of severe punishment.

The enemy wasn't about to wait until we taught our soldiers Hebrew so that they'll be able to understand simple commands. Since I complained to Major Dayan, most foreign volunteers were replaced with Hebrew speaking soldiers instead which were very rare due to casualties. The foreign volunteers, hurriedly transferred to supporting units where understanding direct orders in combat operations were not involved.

The Arab Legion didn't attack yet probably because they didn't know what strategy our forces will follow. They had no idea of the fact that we had no ammunition, not enough to repulse a major attack. They suspected that we'll wait for them to come close to be able to hit them.

However, the cannons didn't stop even for a moment. They covered the terrain inch by inch. Lucky for us, darkness wasn't far away. As soon as it turned dark enough to sneak behind enemy lines, it was easier to overpower sentries and silence cannon crews.

The Legion kept bombarding our positions without mercy, even though none of us were physically there. We were all behind them with commando knifes and bayonets instead of bullets. We killed many of them, eliminating cannon crews quietly, silencing their weapons, including cannons. We took from them plenty of ammunition, enough to face their expected attack during the next day.

That's when Major Dayan's strategy came into play.

We had no tanks to speak of, and the two we had stolen from the British army couldn't be used without ammunition. Major Dayan arranged to get dozens of tractors from neighboring agricultural settlements. They drove back and forth around our positions during the night. The enemy had no idea that these were tractors since the noise was similar to tanks trying to position themselves in the best location for action.

That gimmick apparently convinced the British officers controlling the Arab Legion that our tanks could overwhelm their positions the next morning. When daybreak came about, and no massive attack was eminent, I dispatched a squad to find out what's going on in the Jordanian positions.

It didn't take long for the unit to return and report that all Jordanian positions were abandoned. The tank gimmick worked well, but my men realized that unless we get enough guns and ammunition soon, gimmicks in the future couldn't stop a major attack for long.

Just when our forces everywhere repulsed the combined Arab offensive, the Egyptian forces in the south, the Jordanians in the west, plus the Syrians in the north, United Nations Security Council found it necessary to declare a ceasefire. Someone, somewhere was anxious to give the Arabs a chance to regroup, because now, after capturing some guns and ammunition from our enemies, we could advance and devastate their forces.

United Nations Security Council declared a ceasefire.

Our defense department ordered the military to stop hostilities unless fired upon. Ordered to settle temporarily in Sarafand military base, we were told to keep ourselves busy by refreshing training courses.

The regiment was allotted a platoon of female soldiers. Sergeant Major Eliav was assigned to get the platoon through basic training. Major Dayan figured that since he was a Sergeant Major in the British military he'll be the best qualified to get them through basic training.

The girls, young recruits, treated the sergeant major with their best coaxing calls and names like "honey," "sweetie", "sexy" and so forth, which made training impossible. Because they were females he didn't put pressure on them to obey orders the same way he'd do with men. The result was a total lack of discipline which he failed to handle. After a couple of weeks of disarray the sergeant major suffered a nervous breakdown.

Major Dayan looked for a replacement. Since he couldn't find anyone he believed could handle it, he asked me to take over. Unhappy wasn't the word, but since he had no one else, I had to take the assignment.

On the first day, trying to talk sense to the girls didn't help. They giggled, ignored orders and laughed to their heart content. When Sergeant Benjamin raised his voice and yelled attention, they realized that they couldn't get away with much.

"Attention," Sergeant Benjamin said, "you're soldiers. As such you must obey orders or go to jail - is that clear?"

Mumbling in a chorus was the only response.

The sergeant continued, and pointing to me, he said, "From now on until further notice this is the commanding officer in charge of your training. Disturbances won't be tolerated – no giggling, laughing or talking."

Instinctively, the girls formed a line and stood at attention. Maybe they realized that their new commanding officer won't tolerate lack of discipline.

"At ease. You are here to train – the first lesson would be crawling under barbed wire fences to avoid getting hit."

No one said a word.

Sergeant Benjamin said, "Before your combat training begins I've to whip you into shape. You have to run around the base numerous times. To accomplish that we need squad leaders." He appointed four girls at random as squad leaders despite their objections. "When I say fall in, the squad leaders will form their units. "We'll run now around the base without any equipment. The next round would be running with full equipment, a rifle and a bag on your back. Understood?"

Some of the girls nodded. Most looked mad. Some raised their hand in protest. Sergeant Benjamin was quick to respond. "No protests, objections or suggestions – you are in the army now. The army gives orders and you must obey without question. If you have a complaint you must obey first and complain later to your squad leader – the leader will forward the complaint to me, as your sergeant, and only I will deliver the complaint to the Commander – now, fall in!"

The squad leaders formed four separate units and waited.

"Now, run!"

They started to move but it wasn't a run, it was more like a trot. Sergeant Benjamin raised his voice, "Run faster – left right, left right, faster!"

Acceleration was very slow but they tried to implement the order, which was more than they did when under the command of the sergeant major we replaced.

The next day following the run-around, the girls were ordered to crawl under a barbed wire fence. Since the ground was wet due to recent rains, they tried to avoid contact with the ground. I inspected their performance and because they didn't crawl properly my boot pressed their derrieres downward deeper into the ground. Trying to escape the treatment, many girls scraped their skin as they crawled through.

The intense training forced the girls into a muddy area. They started to complain louder and louder. Upon hearing their complaints, I stopped the training exercise.

"Now listen here: you must learn to lower your body so that when enemy bullets whistle by they won't hit you. If you refuse and disobey instructions, I'll order our machine-guns to open fire. Some of you will sacrifice parts of their rear-ends."

One girl, on the plump side, raised her voice and yelled, "It's against the law to open fire in training – you can't do that!"

"You're mistaken - it's legal to open fire. We are allowed three to seven percent casualties – any of you wants to try it?"

No one responded.

When the order was given to continue the training as scheduled, the girls tried a lot harder. Forcing them to achieve perfection, they had to crawl over and over again until they did it correctly.

This kind of training efforts continued for two full weeks.

Some of the girls went above my head and complained to Major Dayan directly. He listened but didn't promise anything. He didn't ask me to stop either.

At the end of five weeks, training exercises achieved their goal. Despite their complaints, gripes and loud objections, their physical abilities proved that now, after going through enough assimilated combat hardships, they were ready for the real thing.

The cease-fire enabled us to train some of our recruits, but then we faced a big problem internationally: supporters of Israel in the USA realized that America declared an embargo on arms for Israel as well as the Arab countries with the excuse that giving either party military aid, equipment, or ammunition, will prolong the war.

Western nations were all behind the American decision, therefore some supporters of Israel in the USA collected money to help the Israeli side by purchasing a ship called Altalena, stocked it with guns, ammunition and equipment, with an explicit intent of breaking the embargo.

The Arabs didn't need guns or ammunition since Britain and France supplied them generously. The embargo had no effect on them at all. The Israeli military without ammunition and equipment would face total defeat. Why, you may ask: Israeli forces, including old people and women numbered close to fifty thousand. Among them only thirty thousand were physically fit for battle. The Arab forces, Egypt alone, had one million potential soldiers, plus the Jordanian Legion and the Syrian army, not to mention ten other states which declared war, waiting for a chance to join, among them Iraq as well as Libya.

The future looked bleak since Israelis didn't have adequate manpower or the factories to produce guns and ammunition. With the embargo in effect, Israelis would be at the mercy of their enemies, and only a miracle would save them from devastating defeat.

Suddenly, out of the blue, the Soviet Union came to the rescue: they instructed the Check Republic, which at that time was under their control, to supply Israel with all the guns, ammunition and explosives needed. To insure success, they sent ships loaded with oil on credit to refuel the limited equipment Israeli forces possessed during that period.

The Russians, as always, developed policies in opposition to United States preferences. At the same time they announced that any soldier from the Russian armed forces of Jewish extraction was welcome to volunteer and join the Israeli army. Thousands of Russians soldiers, whether Jewish or half Jewish, with some not Jewish at all, were anxious to get out of the Soviet Union, and therefore volunteered, joining the ranks of the IDF. Israel received a flood of Russian artillery specialists, infantry personnel, and many explosive experts who helped to even the balance of power.

This happened while Altalena reached the shores of Israel to unload military equipment and other essential supplies. Again, another surprise: David Ben-Gurion refused to allow Altalena to dock and unload. Later, we found out that the reason was the presence of Menachem Begin, the leader of Etzel, aboard the ship with many of his supporters. If the equipment was to be unloaded, Menachem Begin, Ben-Gurion suspected, could grab the reigns of the government and doom the labor regime. To him, at that period, it seemed more important to deprive Begin from political gains than to repulse the enemy offensives which threatened to exterminate us all.

Consequently, he ordered the Israeli Defense Forces to stop the ship from unloading. Should the Altalena crew refuse to surrender, the IDF was instructed to use as much force as necessary. A direct order reached the Eighth Commando Division to rush to the shore and stop the ship, fire and sink it should resistance intensify. However, while General Itzhak Rabin was willing to oblige, the personnel, mostly Lehi and Etzel members, refused and left their units, including my unit and my regiment. We took all the guns we could find with us to be ready just in case labor will attempt to overpower and perhaps kill Begin. David Ben-Gurion had no problem getting other troops, mostly members of the Hagana under Labor, to do the dirty work. Whether Ben-Gurion wanted to kill Begin and his supporters couldn't be proven, but it certainly looked that way. The Hagana members, labor supporters for the most part, brought in their best weapons, opened fire on the crew and sank the ship, including the equipment therein. Begin escaped, but some of his supporters were killed and wounded.

The country was on the brink of civil war.

The killing and maiming of our brothers and sisters for political gain was hushed up in the belief that it was best kept secret. It's important to note that twice in history ancient Israel lost the independence when similar divisive attitudes were followed. This time most Israelis hoped, the adversaries will have more sense, and reconcile before it's too late.

The Arab states watched the developments with interest.

They waited for a chance to finish whoever the victor will be. Luckily, some leaders, including Begin's men, reached an agreement to settle their disputes rather than physically fight each other, thus jeopardizing the Zionist dream.

CHAPTER FIFTEEN

In order for Israel to win the war they had to acquire heavy tanks. The two tanks the Israeli army possessed were stolen by two British Sergeants who converted to Judaism and married local Jewish girls. They were familiar with the British tanks, and trained Israeli soldiers to use them. The Egyptians had about 400 French medium size tanks. The Jordanians had British tanks, number unknown, as well as the Syrians and the Iraqis which were equipped with heavy duty Stalin tanks.

Two tanks against so many on the enemy side didn't seem to be the best of odds. A desperate search for tanks brought only a trickle. The black market could supply merely junk tanks in need of repairs without cannons or machine-guns. They had to be fitted with heavy machine-guns, a cannon, or missiles. Neither were available.

When the embargo was rescinded by the U.S., the trickle gradually increased. Now, even if the Arabs had enough to attack Israel from every angle, opening two-three fronts at the same time, Israel had almost enough to counter the threats. The Supply of equipment and accessories raised the cost of military needs to the extent that the new state couldn't pay for ammunition.

Factories did their best but they couldn't produce more ammunition than limited quantities. Ammunition for other essential armaments, like heavy machine-guns, cannons and howitzers was desperately needed as well. No matter how much the Israeli manufacturers produced, the troops still had to count their bullets during battles. For instance, as an officer, I had a pistol procured from Second World War stock, restored by Israeli machinists to operate smoothly. The problem was that most officers were given only five bullets to use, plus a British unreliable Stan-gun known to fire at random, regardless of the operator's intentions.

The Israeli Air-Force consisting of four fighter planes had no pilots with experience until foreign volunteers joined: two Jewish pilots, known aces of the Royal Air-Force, just arrived. They trained young Israeli candidates to operate these planes, teaching them the use of instruments, strategic maneuvers, and some tricks of the trade. Later on the young Israeli pilots devised tricks of their own that translated into victories in the air.

Soon, as the boycott against Israel gradually subsided, more tanks were added to Israel's arsenal. Fighter planes, this time of American origin, were added as well. Bombers, in small numbers found their way to the Air-Force, but again, bombs were scarce. Since Israel had bombers they could defend themselves a lot better but they had no ammunition for machine-guns or bombs for the bombers.

Someone among the pilots came up with the idea to use bomb substitutes. They improvised, using seltzer bottles instead of bombs. Whoever heard about it laughed at first and didn't believe substitutes would really work. No other nation in the world managed to use soda bottles so effectively in time of war. The soda bottles when hitting a target, and exploded, made more noise than a real bomb. This trick of the trade was effectively shown in the movie produced about Israel military advances. The movie depicted Frank Sinatra as an Israeli pilot doing just that against Egyptian ground forces in the Sinai desert.

The soda bombs scared the Egyptian infantry units out of their wits. They didn't know what it was and believed that they were facing Israeli secret weapons. The pilots reported that when a soda bottle hit the target they saw Egyptian soldiers running like rabbits in all directions. Such tactics were not duplicated since the Israeli arsenal grew steadily, not only through purchases from foreign suppliers but also from armaments captured from enemy troops.

The Arab Legion, in the meantime, returned to their old positions. They bombarded our defense lines with renewed gusto, making the movement of troops very difficult. The problem was that we did not have enough artillery support as counter balance. Major Dayan listened attentively to complaints about the problem that we had many mortars in our possession, but no ammunition. He promised to do his best and get some.

Later on, we were informed that the three inch mortars we used were manufactured in Israel. Therefore, we assumed they could also manufacture the ammunition for them as well. While the Israeli army advanced quickly in all fronts, the manufacturing was very slow due to lack of manpower. Therefore, the mortars that reached us had no direction devices. They were difficult to operate. We had to guess and estimate the direction of the ammunition when mortars were launched. Furthermore, we were short of ammunition for all weapons in our possession.

Suddenly my field glasses spotted a big truck in a rush to reach our position. We felt sure we'll soon get the ammunition needed to repulse the Arab Legion artillery offensives, and put a stop to them. The truck arrived soon, evading the Jordanian cannons by driving in zigzag. We expected the urgently needed mortar ammunition, but when we opened the first boxes, we were taken aback: the boxes were fully packed with **Bibles!**

Supply of Bibles encouraged the soldiers morale maybe, but we couldn't use them instead ammunition. While the truck left to unload Bibles to other units in that area, our worries intensified: we realized we were playing with fire but had no extinguishers!

Early afternoon, same day, another truck was spotted. This one was smaller than the previous one. Confident that it must be the expected ammunition we waited anxiously, hoping for the best. Imagine the shock on my men's faces when we examine the contents of the truck: thousands of head covers made to be worn in areas where the sun was scorching everything in sight. These hats would be life-savers in the Sinai desert, protecting the troops from sunburns, but again, just like the Bibles, we couldn't use them to stop the Jordanians.

Finally, we received assurances, following direct contact with Major Dayan, that a truck packed with mortar ammunition was on the way scheduled to arrive soon. Indeed, after being bombarded all day and night, the next morning, a huge military truck was seen coming our way. Worries that enemy canons may hit it while we unload created tension. My worry was justified since the enemy cannon crews, apparently noticing the truck, increased their firing frequency.

Like guided by a divine power the cannons blasted the terrain all around the truck, but failed to materialize into a direct hit. Watching cannon blasts with weary eyes, we all prayed that the enemy would miss. Whether the prayers did it or coincidence, we'll never know.

The truck finally arrived.

The cannons intensified their operations. Soon the enemy realized that none of their shells hit the truck. To avoid prolonging the ordeal, I asked for volunteers to unload the ammunition.

No one volunteered.

Since no one volunteered, my order was to unload, clarifying that should they refuse a direct order in time of war, within battle constrains, they'd be subject to Court Martial, thus inviting severe punishment.

No one reacted.

Deciding to encourage my men to unload and show them that there's nothing to fear but fear itself, I climbed on top of the truck. As soon as I reached the top, a cannon shell exploded under the truck, lifting the load and tilting it, causing the ammunition to roll in every direction.

At that moment, losing control, my body rolled along with a constant stream of mortar shells hitting the ground. As it is well known, in order for mortar shells to explode they require two contacts to detonate. The first is when the shell is pushed by the mortar power-bags at the end of the shell. The second contact-hit detonates when the shell hits the ground the second time.

Since the shells hit the ground first the internal detonator was probably activated. They became dangerous to use because when inserted into the mortar pipe the power bags will activate the second detonation and cause it to explode, perhaps kill the crews manning the mortars.

Meanwhile, sprawled on the ground, my right hand was broken in five different places from the elbow down. Beside the pain, the hand turned useless. The medics in my unit prepared a wooden splint, bandaging it the best they knew how, which wasn't very much due to lack of experience, and little medical know-how.

As soon as darkness descended, two squads of my men, including our radio operator, a cute nineteen year old female soldier, just in case the operation will sour, and we'll need to call for support. We called and surprised the Arab Legion. Eliminated most before they realized we were all around them.

Some Legionnaires escaped.

Though we did our best to catch them, our efforts failed. On the way back to our positions, the radio operator tripped and fell, hitting her head against a rock. Hitting her head probably knocked her unconscious so that she couldn't call for help, or make us aware of her misfortune.

By the time we reached our positions, we realized that she wasn't with us any longer. We rushed back to pick her up but we couldn't locate her. Regretfully, we suspected that the enemy found her. Our standing orders were to take with us any soldier, dead or alive, and not leave anyone behind.

It was too late.

There was little we could do. We could launch another assault if we had more troops, enough to support a massive attack which wasn't possible without additional ammunition.

The next day in the afternoon we found out what happened to the radio operator: her body was cut in several parts, like she was a chicken. The breasts were savagely mutilated, her legs severed, her arms cut as well. The body was tossed over to our lines. When we examined her our medical team was convinced that the enemy raped her by the thousands. Experts in that field confirmed that swollen flesh around her private parts was proof of mass rape. Whether they raped her when she was still alive or dead was impossible to tell.

Naturally, the rage level of my men was very high. Many demanded revenge vast and massive. Between demanding and doing was a big difference: with limited supplies we had to give it up for the time being.

Gradually, ammunition and additional weapons reached us as a result of Check suppliers who rushed them over at the insistence of the Soviet Union. Now, we had enough to launch a major offensive against the enemy, devastating them and thus perhaps teach them a lesson. Two company strength forces, mine and a second company commanded by Nissim, a close friend, prepared for an assault against the enemy. We attacked at dawn and pushed the enemy troops out of their entrenched positions on the hill further away from their targeted city, which we assumed was Tel-Aviv. The Legionnaires were hit hard. They scattered and ran, some killed and maimed, mostly trampled while trying to escape.

Once again, the Legionnaires managed to capture Nissim who being wounded was unable to catch up with us following our swift retreat. In order to rescue him we had to be aware of his capture. We were not aware until we counted our casualties, both wounded and dead. When we couldn't account for Nissim, we realized it was too late.

The following day, surprise: Nissim's mutilated body was thrown to our lines, his genitals stuffed into his mouth and secured with tape. This barbaric atrocity was supposed to be an insult against our manhood, I suppose. It was not. It was a deed that toughened our resolve to crush such inhuman scum and eliminate them once and for all.

CHAPTER SIXTEEN

Under pressure from advancing Israeli troops Egyptian forces retreated quickly into the Sinai desert. With a ratio of 100,000 Egyptians to 5,000 Israeli troops it's difficult to understand why. They had better and newer equipment than we did, more manpower, yet they did their best to avoid direct contact.

Several hours later, when the sky turned into a mixture of white and dark grey clouds we guessed they knew about the desert storm coming our way. While other units escorted Major Dayan deeper into the desert, my unit was closer to Gaza Strip held by the Egyptians right in the middle of the major sand storm.

About one in the afternoon the winds began to intensify, the sand lifted, moved freely in the air, hitting mostly the face and the eyes which were more vulnerable than the rest of the body. Forced to stop moving until the storm died down, we were aware that the map of the desert couldn't be relied on. For that reason we had to remember the hill of sand on our left.

Telling my men to seek shelter inside the trucks, I felt sure we'll overcome, possibly ride out the storm unharmed. Sand moved around us violently, hitting the trucks with such force that it made me believe it was something other than sand. In order to protect the vehicle engines, we covered the front of the trucks with tart secured by heavy ropes.

Four and a half hours later the sand storm subsided.

We stepped out of the vehicles cautiously. By now the vehicles were already halfway covered with sand. Before we removed the tarp protection from the part shielding the motors, my men had to remove as much as possible of the sand around in order to enable the vehicles to move. The vehicles couldn't be moved, and the more we tried, the deeper the wheels dug in.

Eating our meals was a painful chore as well.

No matter what, getting rid of the sand that seemed to penetrate the interior of my mouth, was almost impossible. Each time I tried to chew solid food the sand crunched so loud it induced a severe headache. Rinsing the mouth with water from canteens was useless. Sand particles in between the teeth were imbedded in the gums, damaging and hurting delicate tissue.

The only way to solve the problem, was to attack the Egyptian post nearby and take over their positions, which seemed better protected. However, examining the guns, the machine-guns wouldn't fire because the sand saturated every moving part. Our sub-machine guns didn't work either for the same reason. So, taking over the Egyptian positions to improve our condition, couldn't be implemented. We prayed that the Egyptians didn't know about our predicament so that they wouldn't attack and take us over instead.

The best way, it seemed, was to get back to our camp, which shouldn't be too far away. We had to get to it on foot, hoping to gain relief that way. However, the sand hill that was our direction sign, was no longer on the left.

There was something on the right similar to that hill, but than we didn't know for sure what direction would our camp be. From map readings I knew the camp was supposed to be in the north of us, if we could figure where was north. There were no other signs to go by since the sand covered the entire area with a smooth blanket of yellowing granules. The best would be to use a compass. We had one given to me in case of such a development, hoping it would help us find the way out.

Finding the compass was no problem, operating it was a dilemma. The compass pointed to north all right, and we followed for about two hours the pointed direction only to find out that something was wrong with the instrument: we walked around in circles reaching the spot where we left our vehicles in the first place. The compass, as old as much as the equipment we used, didn't work either. Using it may mislead us to walk into enemy territory, perhaps give them a chance to use us for target practice.

Looking ahead, a man-made hill overlooking the Gaza Strip was clearly visible. Since we had no other place to go, we walked as close to it as possible without being spotted. Examining the hill we realized there was no sign of life in it or around it, and that led me to believe that it was deserted. Whether the Egyptians deserted the hill voluntarily or ran away from the approaching storm, we didn't know for sure.

We climbed up the hill cautiously, expecting a surprise. There was no one on the hill. The debris scattered around revealed that the hill was occupied until a short time ago. The debris consisted of pieces of Arab newspaper strips, cigarette butts and food cans discarded with no regard to environment concerns.

Now, convinced that the hill wasn't occupied by anyone, we examined the top as we cleaned the area to make it more hospitable. The hill had zigzag trenches all around, machine-gun positions with several spent slugs decorating the ground, plus torn fabrics ripped by the winds. The only reason for the trenches, including the machine-gun positions, was evidently to prevent Israeli troops from taking over.

Vegetation typical to the desert sprouted in various spots around us. Because we ran out of water and food, we were desperate to find substitutes. Until food and water could reach us, I thought that eating the roots of desert plants like cactuses, may provide us with enough nutrients and moisture to survive until a solution could be found. Besides, the roots of these plants contained the only moisture readily available.

Calling for help wasn't feasible: our communication equipment didn't work either. We couldn't contact our Regiment Commander or our Division Headquarters to report the present conditions on the hill. Nonetheless, I ordered my men to hoist the Israeli flag on the poll.

Maybe we shouldn't have done that.

The enemy would now know that we are here and perhaps attack us to regain the position. Once they recovered from the effect of the storm they might launch a major attack. Should that happen, we'd be in more trouble then we could handle.

We had a dozen or so rifles with limited ammunition. We had sub-machine guns, and lots of hand-grenades. Nothing else. If we're attacked, the hand-grenades may help us repulse only the first stage of an offensive.

Shortly after sunset darkness gradually crept in. So far Egyptian troops refrained from taking action. That was great: the enemy avoided operating under the cover of darkness for unknown reasons. On the other hand, we always attacked at night under cover of darkness, specifically an hour or two before dawn.

The darkness helped us plan a raid to get supplies from the enemy camp. According to our calculations, since headquarters had no idea what's going on with us yet, our best bet to insure our survival was to get enough supplies, equipment and ammunition from the enemy storage facilities.

Because the raid was considered dangerous, we had to be extremely careful. After all, according to my estimation, the enemy had a concentration of two full divisions in Gaza Strip. For that reason we had to depend on volunteers, hoping that we'll have at my disposal at least a dozen men to operate behind enemy lines. Should the volunteers be surrounded, they wouldn't have a chance, not only to complete their mission, but survive as well, and it was doubtful whether they'll be able to return safely to our base. Surprisingly, all my men were eager to volunteer. A unit of twelve men under the leadership of Sergeant Benjamin who, in my belief, had a better handle on discipline than any other.

At three AM the next morning the squad selected left the hill. Covering their faces with dark colored paints, they advanced noiselessly towards enemy positions. When they reached the camp, no more than half a mile away, they stopped to study the sentries' positions. Once the sentries were located, our men silenced them physically with a sudden twist of the neck. One of our volunteers was a young man from Brooklyn who proved to be an expert in twisting necks. He was a big man, equipped with powerful long arms and muscles to match. He was specifically included in the squad due to his expertise to eliminate enemy sentries soundlessly.

Following the sentries demise, the squad entered the camp to assess their next move. The enemy had lots of heavy British machine-guns, small arms, like pistols and rifles, and plenty of ammunition. Next came the requisition of a big truck, loading as much as possible onto it, but first making sure the motor was in working condition.

Once the ammunition and equipment supply problem was solved, the unit located the food warehouse, loaded anything in sight, from vegetables, soups to canned meats to water bottles. Next, Sergeant Benjamin decided to bring an Egyptian general in charge with them in the belief that he'd provide us with essential intelligence.

When they located the general's living quarters, they found him in bed with a woman half his age, which Sergeant Benjamin thought was his wife. We didn't find out the woman's identity until the unit returned, and all goods were unloaded and carried up the hill.

The bewildered general was brought to face me. He was hurriedly dressed, his shirt with his rank on it was halfway tucked in, hanging out of his trousers belt. His dark brown hair was uncombed, his eyes red-rimmed, and his shoes were loosely laced, as though they were merely slippers.

The woman the squad dragged in with him was cowering and shivering close behind him. She had only a thin nightgown on, and no bra. Her breasts dangled as she moved, clearly visible through the transparent nightgown.

"She must be cold," I turned to Sergeant Benjamin. "Get her some warm clothes."

The Sergeant was quick to respond, "Yes, Commander, but we have only men's uniforms."

"Fine, a pair of pants and a shirt should do it."

As soon as the sergeant left I asked the general for his name. Reluctantly, the man said, "Per Geneva conventions I'm not required to reveal more than my name, rank and serial number." His English was heavily throaty and accented, although he did his utmost to conceal it.

"Okay, general, I know that. Your name, please."

"Lieutenant General El-Haramm."

He didn't want to reveal his full name in front of the woman. Perhaps he didn't want her to know his full name for a reason. Could be he gave us an assumed name that we couldn't verify due to the fact that in their rush to bring the general over, they had no time to check documents and identification papers.

"The lady's name, please."

"Fatima," she said, her English accent noticeable.

"Fatima El-Haramm?"

"No, of course not."

"She is not your wife?"

"No, sir, she is not."

Smiling, I asked, "Are you married, general?"

"Yes, sir."

The conversation took on a distinct English tilt. Before that I had to repeat in broken Arabic words recalled from prior question and answer experiences during my service in the Palestine Police. In effect, all I wanted was to find out some facts about the Egyptian forces we faced. While concentrating on my next question, the general's worried voice asked, "Is my wife going to be notified?"

"Notified – about what?"

"Being with this…lady."

Refrained from loud laughter, trying to suppress a giggle, I said, "No, of course not, but only if you answer first a few questions truthfully."

Sergeant Benjamin returned with a pair of Khaki pants and a shirt of the same color. Reluctant to take her nightgown off in our presence, she pulled the pants on top of the gown and the shirt on top of it as well.

The general asked, "What kind of questions?"

"How many troops are under your command?"

The general paused, looked at Fatima, unwilling to talk in with her around. He whispered in my direction, "Forty Five Thousand in the last count."

"Were you planning an attack?"

"Yes, of course."

"Before noon?"

"Sometime in the morning."

"Now that you're here, would the troops attack?"

"Yes, sir."

"Using what weapons?"

"Cannons and heavy machine-guns to soften you up."

"Cannons, general?

Sergeant Benjamin stated, "Sorry, I saw no cannons in the warehouse."

"Cannons are stored in the next warehouse at the end of the camp."

Sergeant Benjamin apologized, "I missed it, Commander. You want me to return to the camp and finish the job?"

"No, no need, it's too late, anyhow."

The general looked at Fatima, his brow furrowing. He seemed worried, perhaps, that she may bear witness to something no general should do: give the enemy details about his troops.

"Any questions, general?"

"Yes, sir."

"Go ahead, ask your questions."

"On the way in I observed only few men on the hill – where are the rest of your troops, Commander?"

I smiled. "That's all there are, general."

He looked stunned. Straightening up, he turned curious, "Is your general here, Commander?"

"What's the purpose?"

"I'd like to talk to him, please."

My sarcastic smile surprised him. "I don't know about my general, but my regiment Commander, Major Dayan, is not here either."

"Major Dayan?"

"Yes, do you know him?"

"I didn't meet him, but I heard of him."

The general seemed to be in a talkative mood. To save time and further questions and answers, my order was that the sergeant will provide separate rooms to accommodate our guests. The information the general provided was vital. Our chances to repulse a major attack wasn't very promising: one battered Israeli company facing two full Egyptian divisions worried me.

We had no chance against the Egyptian troops in direct clashes because of the numbers involved. Since the hill was very steep, we must wait for them to attack and climb to reach us. That seemed the only way to survive a massive attack.

The cannons they intended to use presented the biggest problem. Although the trenches, in zigzag shape, offered some shelter, but if they score a direct hit, the damage will be devastating. The hill was well fortified now that we had two heavy machine-guns with enough ammunition, lots of hand-grenades, plus additional rifles that might help in hitting specific targets, like officers.

CHAPTER SEVENTEEN

The next morning I picked up the binoculars and looked at the amassing troops moving in the distance. It took me several minutes of gaping to realize that the Egyptians slowly but clearly encircled the hill.

Tension buildup tightened every fiber in my body.

By eleven thirty five the same day enemy artillery started to hit different targets on the hill, including a direct hit which knocked the flag down. As soon as it was knocked down, Sergeant Benjamin replaced it with another flag, a lot bigger.

Suddenly, the bombardment stopped.

Usually the enemy would start with softening positions, and therefore, an assault must have been in the offing. With the binoculars viewing all possible directions, the troops didn't seem to move or get ready for an attack. Trying to pin-point the location of the cannons was futile. They probably fired from a greater distance than my eyes could reach. Even if I knew where the cannons were located, there was nothing we could do during the day. Any direct clashes, like hand to hand combat, was out of the question due to number disparity. With their numerical superiority all they had to do is spit on us and we'd probably drown. Sergeant Benjamin appeared at my side. "What d'you think they'll do, Commander?"

"They'll try to take the hill back."

"Maybe retreat," he suggested. "With the numbers we face they could finish us off pretty quick if they attack full force, don't you think?"

"Not really. Sergeant, as long as I'm in-charge and alive, we don't retreat, is that clear?"

Sergeant Benjamin avoided my eyes, he knew we couldn't afford to retreat no matter what. If we abandon the hill, the road to Tel-Aviv will be wide open, even though the hill was in the deep south while the city was way north. With most of the Israeli forces spread thin, engaged all the way in Sinai, deep into Egyptian territories, all units were stretched to the limit. Smarter Egyptian generals could take advantage of the situation, and successfully advance swiftly towards the north.

Artillery restarted the bombardment with renewed vigor. The cannons blasted the hill, chipping and peeling soil from it like a ripe grapefruit. No actual damage, though, since the trenches afforded some shelter from direct hits. The damage was minimal. For two long hours the cannons blasted the hill. We had several wounded, but none were serious injuries. From time to time I heard the rattling of heavy machine-guns but the bullets didn't reach us, which led me to believe that the fire was directed to the side, either left or right.

While cannon fire intensified, layers of Egyptian infantry troops were beginning their advance towards the hill. Having no idea what they wanted to do we worried about the outcome, but if they advanced towards the hill in waves, we eventually will be in trouble.

"Sergeant," I said. "Make sure the machine-guns are ready and the crews have enough hand-grenades. However, don't open fire even if they come closer without my direct order – is that understood?"

"Yes, Commander. I'll inform the men about it."

When the Egyptian troops were about two hundred yards from the top of the hill, tension intensified. What if they came closer from all sides at the same time, and we can't stretch our limited weapons to stop them? They kept on coming slowly, steadily. When they were one hundred yards away we heard the battle-cry in Arabic "Etbach El Yahud!" which meant **kill the Jews**. From time to time the battle cry extended to **"Kill the enemies of Islam."** It sounded strange that an army would encourage their troops in that manner, not kill the enemy, but kill the Jews or the enemies of Islam.

The situation as a whole was weird: the founder and leader of the Palestine Liberation organization, Yassir Arafat, wasn't a Palestinian, he was an Egyptian, born and bred in Egypt. Yet, the Palestinians listened to him and followed him blindly. This led me to believe that this war wasn't a political struggle, it seemed more like a religious war, since both the Palestinians and the Egyptians were Muslims.

"Sergeant, don't forget to warn the men not to open fire without my say so, is that clear?"

"Yes, Commander, I already told them that."

Since we didn't react to their advance the Egyptians were confident they could crush us. Now, they were about fifty yards away. The hill was steeper the closer they came, and only when they were about fifty feet, I raised my hand.

"N o w!" My voice sounded high pitched, loud enough for all to hear, including enemy troops.

The sergeant repeated the command while the machine-guns opened fire, ripping into the bodies of the first enemy layer. Next came the hand-grenades slicing bodies into red meat. With blood flowing everywhere, the hill slope resembled a slaughter house. The first four layers of advancing enemy troops suffered extremely heavy losses.

Watching them with the binoculars, to my surprise, many of the remaining layers turned and ran in the opposite direction. In the distance, I saw a line of commissioned and non-commissioned officers prod the troops, using bayonets and commando knives to force them to advance. Despite our concentrated fire the officers pushed many to face us, ignoring the fact that our machine-guns cut them down faster than a giant lawn-mower cutting grass. The lower part of the hill looked red with bodies. The prodding didn't persuade the troops to go ahead and die. They definitely didn't want to die. They turned and ran, knocked the officers down, trampling many of their own comrades into oblivion.

The Egyptians panicked and retreated further south, just like in a stampede. Suddenly, they stopped, apparently forced to regroup by Egyptian troopers that appeared behind, threatening them with bodily harm. In my estimation, at least eight or nine thousand Egyptian soldiers joined their maker that day. Maybe more. The Egyptian troops froze, caught between their own troops forcing them to advance, and our merciless machine-gun fire, pressing them to flee or die.

That's when Major Dayan returned from Sinai Desert. Upon hearing the echoes of fire, he rushed to see what's going on. He blocked the rear of the regrouping Egyptians, preventing their reorganization. Before anyone realized what's happening, Major Dayan's two full companies surrounded the entire Egyptian force, giving them a chance to surrender or die.

Now, as the battle was finally over, we faced the problem of keeping the Egyptian troops with us until the army reached our positions to take them to a prisoner's camp in the rear. Keeping the enemy troops under normal conditions wouldn't be a problem, but since we hardly had sufficient food and water for our own forces we had to give them the minimum possible to keep them alive. That's when it came to me that our enemies were either stupid or irrational fanatics. On my first inspection tour to see whether we can make it easier for them to tolerate the harsh conditions, I walked along the long line of barbed wire. We walked, examining their filthy blood covered uniforms, when an Egyptian sergeant raised his voice, labeling us a disgrace to the civilized world, complaining about the way we treated prisoners. He seemed to understand some English and for that reason I approached the barbed wire fence.

"What exactly is your problem, sergeant, may be I can help?"

Instead of an answer, he spat in my face twice followed by curses in colorful Arabic. I wiped off the saliva from my cheek with the sleeve on my shirt, ready to lecture him on decency, when Sergeant Benjamin noticed he got ready to spit again, lifted his rifle butt and hit him on the top of his head. The Egyptian sergeant collapsed, moaning, clutching his injured skull.

"Sergeant Benjamin, you shouldn't have done that," I said. "I might have succeeded to make him understand that under the present circumstances we did our best."

Sergeant Benjamin didn't smile. "I doubt it, Commander," he said. "The only thing he understands is the pain inflicted to his head. Suppose you were a prisoner in Egyptian hands and you did what he did – what d'you think would have happened?"

"I'd probably be in heaven, I'm sure."

"Then, why bother?"

"I'm not used to it, sergeant. The biblical King Solomon's saying doesn't apply any more."

"Which saying was that?"

"When you meet a **hungry man, give him food** – when you meet a **thirsty man, give him water**."

The sergeant smiled. "Here's another saying, Commander, **spread your bread above the water** which amounts to the same thing: meaning if you treat your enemy nicely, the enemy would reciprocate – but, this doesn't apply to our present enemies – if you treat them nice they believe you are either weak or a coward."

The brief exchange of words with Sergeant Benjamin was interesting and true. We got rid of the British and yet, now we are facing Egyptians influenced by a fanatic religion that believes the sword is the only solution to all their problems.

CHAPTER EIGHTEEN

Samson in the Old Testament, President Clinton in USA, and others, although strong in many other ways, were weaklings when challenged by beautiful females. Moshe Dayan, though not facing similar circumstances, developed a weakness he couldn't control. Although this fact was not acknowledged and definitely not verified by Dayan himself, he took a chance many times, and once, even endangered his life and the welfare of the units he commanded in order to meet a female soldier he was sweet on.

During that period, Israel had few helicopters. They were used for military purposes only. Moshe Dayan commandeered a helicopter to meet a female soldier inside Egyptian territory. He took the biggest chance of his life but refused to talk about it. The helicopter was almost shot down by enemy anti-aircraft fire. The rendezvous took place, but on the way back the helicopter was hit, the engine crippled, and if not for the pilot's experience, dexterity and courageous maneuvers, his life would come to a bitter end. Since much depended on his strategic planning, Israel's future military achievements would have been lost.

Very few people knew about that particular escapade. He never mentioned it, so whether it really happened there is no way to tell. However, many believed the saying that **where there's smoke there is fire**.

Such behavior didn't diminish his talent as a military genius. Whether anyone approved of his character made little difference. Commanding only a regiment of fifteen hundred men, ill-equipped and heavily outnumbered, he managed to defeat vast Egyptian forces in every battle and encounter, mostly due to his strategic planning and tactics. It goes without saying that the devotion of the foot soldiers added to his success. Many believed Israel's victories against such odds were definitely miracles. Whether miracles decided success or failure no one knew, but Moshe Dayan himself believed that the human element and his strategies did it. The regiment's subordinates believed in him, trusted his leading abilities, and obeyed him blindly.

Moshe Dayan's way of planning a coming battle was simple: he called a conference of all officers into a big tent showing the military map of the terrain. The terrain was marked on that map with extensive details showing hills, valleys, even trees. He explained what the target meant to the entire front, pointing out dangerous locations and the means to overpower them..

It amazed me that the man with one eye only, the other eye was lost when he acted as a scout for the Australian army in Syria during The Second World War, he saw clearer and better than all of us put together who were blessed with two good seeing eyes. The black patch over the socket of the missing eye became a symbol of military superiority around the globe. He had lots of offers from volunteers to provide him with a seeing living eye for the empty socket. However, doctors ruled against it because the bone was fractured beyond repair, and the nerve endings were in very bad shape. Medical experts decided it'd be futile even to try since the sniper shattered the socket beyond repair when he hit the eye through the binoculars. Nothing, they all concluded, could be done to restore his eye or even hold an artificial eye in place.

He was able to figure ways to win battles that none of us thought of. One strategy was to hit a target from three sides, thus scatter enemy forces to defend the sectors under attack. The major assault came from a side that no one expected. The same strategy was used successfully by American forces in the first Iraqi war.

With a force of two full companies, company number one, mine, and company number two, commanded by another captain I didn't meet yet. The plan repeated in the battle for Beer-Sheva in the Negev was occupied by four Egyptian regiments in full gear, well equipped and with enough supplies for a little more than a division. All the Egyptian supplies were hidden well underground. Numerous warehouses with food and canned meats, soups of all kinds as well as bread were enough to last them, in case of a siege, at least six months.

My company reached the top of the hill across from the city early dawn. We had three inch mortars only with adequate ammunition. However, we had no direction devices since the factory in Ramat-Gan lacked manpower to manufacture them.

The crews had little training to operate mortars, and no ammunition for cannons even if we had any. The position of mortars behind the hill had no direct visibility of the target. The crews had to rely on instructions from the command post which also served as the observation center.

From the top of the hill, deeply trenched in the ground for maximum safety, my contact with the crews down the hill was via phone wires. Mortars as a rule were mainly used to overwhelm the enemy with scattered fire, thus causing anxiety and panic.

The first mortar was directed to hit right of the target. The second directed to hit the left, while the third mortar directed to the middle. After the directions were established by trial and error, the fire was successive, devastating entire sections of the city like a heavy shower in the Israeli winter.

Since the mortars had no direction devices, the pipe (mortars are made from metal pipes, in this case three inches wide) was held by a member of the crew, while the ammunition was dropped in where contact with the first detonator usually took place. Once the detonator was activated inside the pipe, the power pack (usually five-six bags filled with gun-powder) would ignite and produce enough gases to force ammunition out towards the target. For longer distance the maximum number of gun-powder bags were attached to the lower part of the ammunition. For shorter distances, less bags were used, depending on the distance required. The activated mortar ammunition was lifted into the air, curled over to the other side of the hill, hitting the target. Once the target was hit, it would explode, causing extensive damage on the ground.

We saturated the terrain so that all the cannons they had ready for action were heavily damaged. Most commanders of the Egyptians forces were caught by surprise. Whoever tried to reach either cannons or howitzers were hit, rendering them defenseless. By morning, we entered the city itself, and meeting no resistance, enabled us to take the general in-charge into custody as well.

While my company entered the city to secure the area, the megaphones from different parts of the hill urged the enemy to surrender. The answer to that was a hail of machine-gun fire. We notified Major Dayan about the answer. The major divided the second company into two equal forces, encircled the city, leaving only one way to escape through the valley controlled by our troops.

The megaphones urged the enemy to surrender once again. Although they were headed for an obvious defeat, they opened fire for the second time. This time company number two returned fire.

The Egyptian troops disintegrated, tried to flee, running straight into the firing range of our own machine-guns. The result was pitiful. Whoever wasn't dead or wounded, had been taken prisoner. Since our own food supplies were depleted, we survived on salty herrings, the only food left in our possession. Having limited supplies of water as well, eating herrings three times a day created lots of problems.

We were made aware by the captured general about their underground warehouses. Major Dayan decided to use Egyptian foods as substitutes to the herring-diet as well as liquids they called soft drinks. Big quantities of meat cans and soft drinks were provided to the troops as well as to the prisoners. The prisoners consumed everything with no complaints. They seemed to enjoy them.

Hesitant, my men tried the meats first.

The taste was far from pleasing our taste buds, but their meats were superior to our herring-diet. The soft drinks had the flavor of discarded water, perhaps because they were too warm to quench thirst. That's when we discovered that Egyptians had plenty canned soups available as well. I took one sip of the soup, and didn't believe it: the taste was so bad forcing us to rinse our mouths for hours, first to eliminate the taste, next to get rid of the odors killing our taste-buds inside our mouths.

As soon as Beer-Sheva was secured, we handed the town over to our infantry units. We had orders to follow the Egyptians into Sinai Desert and dismantle staging areas for attacks against our forces.

Since many other units advanced into Egyptian territory, we had to slow down not to overtake them. For that reason, we had orders to camp for a day or two. The problem was that desert climate didn't always cooperate with military operations: during the night temperatures hit below zero. During the day the heat was so high that if you dropped an egg on the sand it'll be cooked in no time.

In the evening, most men in my company decided to prepare for a good night's sleep. Due to lack of tents, we were provided with brand new sleeping bags. The sleeping bags had a zipper to the length. The user was able to zip the bag from the inside as well as open it when the sleeping period was over.

Some of my men were dozing off, most were already sleeping. Despite the freezing temperature the interior of the bag provided enough heat to make the user comfortable. Whoever invented the sleeping bags took everything into consideration except answering an important question: what if the zipper gets stuck? Nobody knew the answer yet, but around two after midnight the question demanded an immediate resolution.

Since I was sound asleep, I believed nothing would disturb my rest except the sound of firearms. Several minutes after two in the morning I heard shots echoing in the night. True, we had two sentries on guard just in case an enemy patrol would dare come by, but being the company commander, I had to get out of the sleeping bag quickly, and find out what's happening before it turned into a dangerous complication.

Trying to open the zipper repeatedly, realization struck: the zipper was stuck. My nerves reminded me that an enemy patrol might come by, spray enough fire to hit the sleeping bags and eliminate to entire company before we could figure how to get out. Having no other way to open the bag, I pulled my commando knife, and slashed the fabric from top to bottom.

As soon as I was out of the bag the freezing temperature hit me hard: my underwear froze first, my nose warned me to cover myself and my lips released lots of vapor. Investigating the nature of the shots, the sentries stated that they saw something moving in the vicinity. To be on the safe side, they both opened fire to prevent harming the sleeping soldiers.

Shivering despite the cover of blankets on top of the uniform, I was able to ascertain that there was no enemy patrol in the area. The sentries imagination triggered the shots, scarring the daylights out of many. However, all my men succeeded to open the zippers with no trouble except me.

Trying to get back into the sleeping bag was impossible. Without a functioning zipper the bag had no value. Unable to sleep a wink, although I covered myself with anything within reach, including another layer of heavy socks for my feet, warming up was only a dream.

While most Israeli forces remained static, and Egyptians counter-attacked in an effort to break through our defenses, no one in the wide world expressed concern. Now, that the enemy failed in all their offensives, and we moved the war into Egyptian territories, United Nations, even United States, raised hell, anxious to stop the war. The Security Council voted to impose another one-sided cease-fire. The excuse was that the cease-fire will save civilian lives.

Moshe Dayan's regiment, my company included, was ordered to dig in, wait and observe the cease-fire until further notice. Many of our generals disagreed. It took lots of casualties to repulse our enemies in all fronts. Stopping the military push now without enemy surrender only meant that our forces will have to sacrifice more troops in order to repulse future attacks.

To enable our forces hold the area where they were, Division Command rushed supplies of tents, blankets and beds. My tent, separate from the others, had all basic needs to satisfy the troops under the circumstances, including a pillow to rest the head on.

The first night was uneventful.

The next morning on my way for breakfast I saw one of my subordinates walk barefoot on the sandy terrain, dragging his boots behind him on a string. From time to time he talked to the boots as if they were alive. Realizing that I watched him, he stopped and said, "Hold it, I have a headache, don't bark so loud!"

"What d'you think you're doing, soldier?"

"I'm going to have breakfast, Commander."

"Why d'you drag the boots?"

"That's my dog, Commander, he has to eat too."

Many soldiers tried from time to time to secure a discharge from the army that way, hoping to be recognized by medics as mentally unstable. This one overdid it. "Playing games won't help you, soldier. Put your boots on and stop the nonsense - it's an order, you understand?"

"I'm not pretending, Commander."

"You can't go barefoot to the dining-room to eat. The kitchen has orders to serve only personnel who follow the rules: you must be properly dressed, and clean-shaven. Besides, no pets are allowed."

"But, Commander, I'm…"

"No buts, soldier. When you finish breakfast with your boots on, report to the regiment medic – he'll treat any problem you may have, understood?"

"Yes, Commander, but I'd like to say…"

"Don't - are you refusing a direct order, soldier?"

"No, Commander."

"Very well then, put your boots on, don't argue."

He rushed to slip his feet into the boots without socks. "Can I go now, Commander?"

"Don't wear your boots without socks. Go back to your tent, put the socks on first, is that clear?"

Reluctantly, he said, "Yes, Commander."

Impressing him that I was serious, I said, "If I see you again without socks or boots, you'll be in trouble, remember that!"

He left.

As I headed for the officers dining tent, my stomach objected to additional delays. Whether he listened to my advice or not and put his socks on was impossible to tell. I didn't see him since. Even if I did I had enough problems of my own, and definitely wasn't in the mood to look for more.

One of the biggest problems hit me the day after, as I was trying to get off the bed. The sharp pain, like a needle prick, spread slowly throughout my left knee. To ease the pain, treating it like an itch didn't help. Since it was dark inside the tent, it was difficult to see clearly. Something about three feet long crawled on the floor, wiggling out of the tent. It looked like a snake. The Sinai Desert had plenty of rattlesnakes. A close examination of the affected knee my eyes concentrated on the reddish mark on the side of the knee. It looked swollen, irritated and injured. Watching the knee for a minute, at which time it seemed to me that the mark turned black, developing a reddish ring around it, appeared to spread rapidly up and down the leg.

Sergeant Benjamin walked by as I came out. "Call the medic, sergeant, please."

The regimental medic came sixteen minutes later, had one look at my exposed knee and dismissed all my fears, advising me not to panic.

"That's nothing, Commander. Probably a bee sting."

By that time the black mark got bigger, the reddish ring spread as well. "I had bee stings before, doc, this isn't one."

He laughed. "Who is the medic here, Commander, you or me?"

The irritation increased to the extent that I felt like scratching. Telling him so didn't change his mind. Instead he lectured me about bee stings, trying to convince me that he was the only authority on the subject in the regiment. Objecting to his sermon, my insistence that I had experience with bees didn't do much good either. Besides, having doubts whether bees could thrive in desert conditions seemed to agitate him. As a result, he raised his voice to make his point just when a military jeep slowed down and stopped next to us. The driver, a major, didn't appreciate the medic's diagnostic abilities.

The major looked at the knee, listened to the medic's opinion and explanations, and despite his attempts to restrain himself, he couldn't keep quiet for long. "You idiot," the major said. "This is a rattlesnake sting. It's a deadly snake bite – help him into the jeep and be quick about it!"

Surprised at the major's diagnostic dexterity, he said, "Yes, major. But how can you tell, sir?"

"I'm the Commander of the field hospital medical team, I've seen many similar snake bites in the desert – if it's not treated at once he could lose his leg."

"Sorry, major, I didn't know."

These were the last words reaching my eardrums when the jeep moved forward at high speed, spitting sand behind as acceleration pushed the vehicle vigorously ahead. Apparently, the major was right: the black mark spread faster, and the inflamed area now covered the knee almost completely.

Several hours later, waking up in the field hospital, my left leg was tied, strung up to the ceiling. The knee was bandaged tightly and the leg felt heavy and uncomfortable.

The fuzzy face of a young nurse was the first I saw when my eyes strained to focus, looking up. She had a needle filled with liquid in her hand, smiled and said, "It's time for another shot, does the leg still hurt?"

"Yes, it does – what's the shot for?"

Trying to avoid an answer, she concentrated on the shot, squirted some liquid upwards to ensure it worked, and before I could say anything else, she rapidly stuck the needle, holding it tightly until the tissue was penetrated, saturating the muscle. When the needle made contact it felt more like a knife cut. Feeling certain she hit bone, not muscle, my voice turned loud, "Nurse, I asked you a question – why do I need that shot?"

"Doctor's orders," she said. "I have to give you a shot every hour until further notice," and trying hard not to listen to questions, she walked out fast leaving me no time to react.

CHAPTER NINETEEN

While our division was busy in the Negev mopping up remnants of Egyptian forces, the battle for Jerusalem was in full swing. The problem was that the City, new and old, was situated on top of the mountain. The Jordanian army had a big advantage.

That's about the time that Colonel Mickie Marcus, an American volunteer who donated his time and expertise to help write the military manual for the Israeli defense forces, called for short IDF, arrived and began to write. The movie produced about him in Hollywood, however, didn't present the factual truth about his death.

When Colonel Marcus arrived on the scene he sat down with Israeli officers, and prepared a plan to overcome enemy interference when attempts to drive up the mountain were made. The road excavated enabled gradual advance without being stopped by enemy fire. Colonel Marcus, urged and inspired the troops, that's true, but even that wasn't as fast as the plan called for.

The mountain, too steep to go straight up, forced Israeli troops to excavate the road around and around the mountain in strips. That way, enemy scouts couldn't tell where the road was turning, since they were shielded from direct view.

Nowadays, tourist-travelers can still witness the wiggling road from the bottom to the top. Many destroyed trucks, enemy armored vehicles, are still decorating parts of the road. Finally, Israeli troops could reach the top of the mountain to counter Jordanian attempts to stop them. Once they reached the top, Jordanian troops vacated the area. Trying to minimize their casualties, the Jordanians retreated, a typical move whenever Israeli troops advanced too fast for them to react.

From that point onward, Israeli troops advanced rapidly into the old city, eliminating pockets of resistance one by one until the entire city was free and secure. The Western Wall, also known as the Wailing Wall, the physical remnant of King Solomon's Temple mentioned in the Old Testament, was filthy, along with many Christian Churches which were used by the Arabs as latrines. They were aware that these were holy sites of other faiths. That didn't matter to the Muslims obviously, since the desecration and the stench, in many locations, was unbelievable, and unbearable.

The most disappointing fact was that no nation in this enlightened world protested the despicable desecration of holy places by Muslim Palestinians in Jerusalem. The cleanup of the old city required massive efforts. However, at the end, it was accomplished.

These days, Jerusalem's old city is clean, improved and preserved, and people of all faiths, including Muslims who desecrated sites before, have free access, encouraged to visit whenever they wish. The only restriction is for violent people, like terrorists, whose only goal in life was and still is to make others miserable.

Most units in Jerusalem used the British inferior Stan-Guns which fired intermittently, but not when actually needed. Captain Uzi, the Commander of a company in Jerusalem, had the misfortune of facing the same dilemma with his unit many times. He took the Stan-Gun apart and examined it only to ascertain that it had too many moving parts. When the parts got dirty, the gun didn't work well. Whenever he had a spare moment, he thought about it. He put together a small weapon without moving parts. He tested the new assembled sub-machine-gun by sticking it in the mud, lifting it up and firing. He tried that several times, and it worked well. This was the first Uzi sub-machine gun as we all know it nowadays used by the US secret Service, the European Union security services and many others. The Uzi sub-machine-gun gradually replaced the British Stan-Gun. As a result, all pockets of enemy fire eventually were eliminated.

About the same time, Colonel Marcus worked hard on the military manual. The tragedy was that enemy personnel were still scattered around, forcing Israeli troops to guard crossings and strategic areas. The Colonel didn't speak Hebrew, and that sealed his fate. At that time, with hygiene difficult, field latrines were used. One evening, wishing to relieve himself, he left a secure area and told the armed guard at the crossing about it. The guard happened to speak English and there was no problem there.

However, when he returned about twenty minutes later, the guard changed. This one was a Yemenite Jew. He didn't know English. He had no idea of Yiddish, the language practiced by

European Jews in exile. Furthermore, he never heard of the Colonel. That made the situation perilous for Colonel Marcus since he was somewhat conversant in Yiddish but had no knowledge of Hebrew, except maybe words like "Shalom", and "Mazal Tov".

When he reached the crossing, the guard yelled, "Stop - password!"

The Colonel didn't grasp the meaning of the words and replied in Yiddish, "Hey, you know me, I'm Colonel Marcus, don't you remember?"

"Stop," the guard screamed, "or I shoot!"

The Colonel tried to respond in English to the guard. Apparently, the guard thought he might be British. "Don't move, you hear?"

Colonel Marcus didn't know that the guards changed while he was away. Perhaps he believed it was a joke. He kept advancing towards the guard's position while still zipping up his pants. That's the moment the shot rang out. The Colonel collapsed, hitting the ground with a thud. He didn't move or utter a sound, not even a moan. The shot brought the sergeant in-charge on the double, and when he saw the bleeding body of Colonel Marcus on the ground, he realized what happened.   .

"Dammit, you killed him!"

"I warned him," the guard said, "he sounded British."

"This is Colonel Marcus, private, he is one of ours!"

The guard, not knowing who the Colonel was, wasn't impressed. Apparently, while the guards changed, the password changed as well. Even if he knew the prior password, no one could have given him the new password.

The loss of Colonel Marcus was painful. There was little the military could do to rectify it. Blaming the guard would be useless. Blaming without cause never helped anybody.

CHAPTER TWENTY

Falujah Pocket, a man made hill in the south, was the stronghold of the Egyptian army amidst several small Israeli agricultural settlements. The hill was surrounded by a vast field saturated with personnel field mines to prevent Israeli troops from using the surprise element.

The Egyptians had about three thousand troops, thirty known German high ranking SS officers on their side, advisors for Gamal Abdul Nasser, the highest ranking enemy officer in the area, who planned to take over southern Israel.

The SS officers, entrenched in the British Police Fort at the foot of the hill, a stone building designed to increase security, were supposed to train the Egyptian troops, advise their officers in battle strategies in an effort to outsmart and overpower the Israeli army.

Intelligence reports revealed that the Egyptians and the Germans who volunteered to help them, were well equipped, well trained and smarter than the run-of-the-mill Egyptian soldiers who didn't stand much of a chance against dedicated Israeli soldiers.

It was still quite dark at dawn when we started to move. We had two companies in the area with orders from Major Dayan to deploy around the East, facing the hill, and wait for the third company if and when available, since they were busy elsewhere. He neglected to tell us about the field mines surrounding the hill. That was a drawback: the mines were well camouflaged, almost impossible to detect.

To make sure there were no mines on the way to the foot of the hill, I ordered my men to use sub-machine gun fire aimed at the ground to activate them. These were standing orders in similar situations. I always made certain that we carefully implemented them.

Since we had to cross about two hundred feet of field mines infested territory, we stepped cautiously towards the hill. Sub-machine-gun fire at the ground was effective, but should we miss one or two was my biggest worry. Stepping ahead first, showing the men there's nothing to fear if they were careful, advising them to fit their footsteps in my tracks just in case mines were still present in the ground.

The men gained confidence when they realized that we were already halfway to our destination, and all was well. That's when it happened: the second man in the company walking behind me lost his footing for a split second and hit a field mine: the explosion, loud and devastating, ripped his leg to a point below the knee. The blood flow aggravated our situation since we had to stop amid the mine field. We did our best to handle the bleeding before we moved on.

Following the incident, we slowed down considerably, and now, even though it was still within dawn, the enemy might see us, perhaps open fire. We didn't know why they waited that long: we almost reached the foot of the hill when the enemy discovered our presence. Two men were hit: one in the right shoulder, the other in the thigh.

Dawn became early morning and visibility improved to the extent that the fire from the Police Fort, where the German officers were entrenched, intensified. We were forced to crouch low to avoid getting hit. The first consideration was to stop the fire coming from the fort. We tried to blast the fort walls with dynamite to no avail. The fort, built with rock blocks, was much too thick for regular doses of explosives. I contacted artillery for support, ask to poke some holes in the fort so that we may perhaps enlarge them with additional dynamite.

Our artillery responded quickly.

For about fifteen minutes the Police Fort, pounded heavily from all sides, yielded no results. Once again two men were dispatched to attach a bigger dynamite pack at the foot of the building. On their return, we detonated the dynamite by remote control. The explosion was so powerful that we felt the earth shake for a few seconds. This time the rock block chipped. At this rate, we may accomplish our mission in a week or two.

Two weeks delay was out of the question.

The SS men kept firing. Reporting the situation to headquarters didn't do much good. Instructions urged us to halt all attempts until we get the new ammunition now on the way. The problem was that by that time it was already late afternoon. Darkness gradually impaired visibility. I didn't want to waste any explosives on trial and error. I hoped that the new ammunition would help us.

The machine-gun ammunition arrived in three boxes. It was delivered to the gunners in charge. However, to avoid difficult conditions my men were ordered to wait for morning clarity before another try. To make sure it was the right ammunition, machine-gun crews examined it closely. They reported a strange odor emanating from it. The puzzling odor raised questions with reference to the ammunition's qualitative aspect.

Checking whether there was anything wrong with the ammunition, I noticed that the tops of the bullets were covered with a layer of clear material, similar to plastic coating. The smell reminded me of tear-gas. Apparently, when the lead would hit the target, the friction of making contact will activate tear-gas release into the air, impairing enemy eyesight. In order to avoid complications, I checked with headquarters to make sure and verify my conclusions.

Being informed that the machine-gun bullets were indeed tear-gas tipped ammunition intended for use against the German SS officers, the handling of the Police Fort was actually labeled a Police action.

Using tear-gas in any form was acceptable to dislodge criminals from their hideout. Nazis, per our understanding, were not considered soldiers but dangerous criminals. When we used the new ammunition we had to make sure that the bullets hit the hole chipped by the cannons so that the tear-gas will penetrate the interior of the building. Since the SS men had no gas-masks, I assumed, they'll come out and probably surrender.

Entrenched for the night, the men planned a long rest, ready to take advantage of an invigorating sleep. However, around midnight, just as we were dozing off, a big number of Egyptian soldiers jumped into our trenches, and before we realized what's going on, many of my men had their earlobes, noses and cheeks bitten and bleeding.

Apparently, biting was easier for them because in close proximity the Israeli soldiers were superior, and much more effective. Fearing that using firearms or knives will alert the rest of us, they preferred bites instead. Since our expertise didn't extend to biting, and the odor of the Egyptian bodies alerted us as to the presence of the enemy, we used our hands as well as Stan-gun butts to fight them off.

Even in the dark of night my men managed to overpower the assaulting Egyptian troops. Many Egyptians were killed, lots of them suffered painful injuries, while some escaped without a scratch. Moans and groans on both sides dominated the scene. The majority were taken prisoners needing medical attention were transferred to the rear where they were treated, restrained and incarcerated.

Sleepless, tired and grouchy, we faced the approaching new day. Daylight, instead of being a welcome occurrence with new opportunities, was a heavy burden. The sight of bandaged noses, earlobes and cheeks, tiny white decorations, wasn't an encouraging sight. When combined with crumbled uniforms, we seemed more like a bunch of civilians, but definitely didn't look like soldiers.

Our uniforms were a collection of several foreign armies: British battle-dresses, French trousers, American shirts plus boots of various other nations. The orders to remove officers ranks from the shoulders made it impossible to distinguish between officers and privates. The idea was to make it difficult for enemy snipers to hit and kill Israeli officers.

As soon as we opened our eyes long enough to stop squinting against the morning sun, we opened fire with machine-guns, using the new ammunition. The bullets hitting the fort forced tear-gas into the building for about half an hour. An hour or so later, as expected, a white flag appeared at the entrance of the building followed by thirty SS officers, gas-masks covering their faces, their hands high up in the air. These SS officers were quick to kill others, but when it came to their own mortality, they surely didn't want to die.

The tear-gas accomplished more than cannon fire and machine-gun fire. Apparently, they were ready for gas use but not fast enough using the masks. Once they inhaled the tear gas, putting the gas mask on wasn't effective at all. The Germans, facing Israeli soldiers for the first time in their lives, seemed shocked. The military facing them didn't look like a military unit to them. The Germans uniforms were pressed, the shoes shinning like mirrors, their whiskers trimmed, and faces clean shaven.

Compared to them, the Israeli soldiers looked more like a militia band.

We never saw real life Germans either. They looked exactly like in the movies, and I was amazed that even in captivity they were meticulous about appearance and military protocol. One of the German officers, his chest full of colorful decorations, his shoulders an array of rank designations, requested to see the commanding officer. Sergeant Benjamin pointed to me. The German general looked skeptically in my direction.

I heard the exchange of words.

"Is he the officer in-charge?

"Yes, that's our commander."

Escorted by Sergeant Benjamin, the SS general, and he had to be a general judging by all these decorations on his uniform, was brought before me. He stopped in front of me looking somewhat shaken to see an enemy that didn't look like an enemy, or a soldier of any kind.

Regardless of his feelings, the salute he honored me with was a proper military greeting. The eyes straight ahead, the step firm and the click of the shoes as military as shown in the movies. I dismissed his salute with a shrug, and asked, "What's your problem?"

"Are you the Division Commander, sir?"

"No. I'm the Company Commander."

"I'd like to see the officer in charge, please, sir."

"That's me."

Incredulous, he asked, "Is the Division Commander available?"

"No. We don't have a Division Commander here."

"I'd settle for the highest rank, sir."

"The highest rank around is the Regiment Commander."

His face brightencd.

It seemed to me that he'd like to see anyone but me. He wasn't happy with my uniform, my behavior and my disposition.

"I'd see the Regiment Commander if you don't mind, sir."

"Major Moshe Dayan is busy elsewhere."

"D-a-y-a-n?" he stretched the pronunciation of the name, giving me the impression that he heard of him, yet didn't seem to like him either.

"Yes. Major Dayan."

The General hesitated for a few seconds, and said, "You're the only one available, sir?"

"Yes, is there a problem?"

His voice an octave higher, he said, "I'm the highest ranking officer among the prisoners. I'm entitled to speak to the highest rank."

"Hold it, I'm the highest rank here right now. Speak up or go back."

His cheeks reddening, he looked me over with distrust. "I'd like to inform you that the conditions we're kept in are not fitting our military ranks. We're entitled…"

"You're prisoners. That's the best we can do under the circumstances for now – is that all?"

His eyes narrowed when he raised his voice, "We must be treated according to Geneva Conventions, sir, and I'd like to inform you…"

"If that's all, go back. Don't waste my time."

"Sorry if you think so, sir, but I insist…"

The short sleeve shirt I had on exposed the arms, and when he looked closely, he was surprised to see that none of us had any green numbers like European Jews had, the ones they herded into their concentration camps. "Insist, my foot," I raised my voice. "You're lucky I have orders to keep you alive. If it's up to me your body parts will be a plastic bag, do you understand me, general, whatever your name is?"

I could tell he hated me. But, apparently, he was pleased that we had no green numbers on the arms, otherwise maybe he feared his life wouldn't be spared. He wasn't too happy, though, to be scolded by an enemy officer who didn't seem to be like an officer he pictured an officer to be.

CHAPTER TWENTY ONE

Following the capture of thirty SS officers, whereas Colonel Gamal Abdul Nasser, the man in charge of the Egyptian forces in Falujah Pocket, the orders were specific: attack and eliminate enemy troops controlling the hill.

By dawn the next day, all three companies were ready to start. Major Dayan, studying the maps, concluded that the best way to attack was from three sides. Artillery softening was requested, as well as intensified backing when our troops will climb the hill and try to dislodge enemy units from their entrenched positions. Per official intelligence reports reaching us, we understood that the enemy held heavily fortified positions, making dislodging said troops extremely difficult.

Difficult or not, Major Dayan ordered to follow his plan and attack. The tree prong assault designed to overwhelm the enemy was a must. The same tactics worked before successfully.

Company number three attacked from the rear. First came machine-gun fire, followed closely by a barrage of hand-grenades, sub-machine guns and rifles. At the same time company number one, my own company, attacked similarly from the North, while company number two, attacked from the South. Squeezed from three sides, enemy troops decided to try to ease the pressure by escaping through the front. What the enemy wasn't aware of is that this was the plan from the start: the front was covered by two heavy machines-guns. While the maneuvers continued, artillery kept softening the hill with frequent cannon hits, which demoralized, killed, and confused Colonel Nasser's men.

Since the enemy raised white flags, indicating surrender, Major Dayan ordered a temporary cease-fire. The surrendering Egyptian troops were surrounded, kept under guard, pending official instructions from Prime Minister David Ben-Gurion, who doubled as Defense Minister during that period.

Ordered to drop the weapons into a pile, including ammunition, enemy personnel hesitated. They were allowed to consult each other and reach a decision. Fearing repercussion, the prisoners obeyed. Colonel Gamal Abdul Nasser, the commander in charge was first to drop his pistol, his commando knife as well as all his ammunition into the pile as well. Shortly thereafter, a direct order from the Defense Ministry was issued to release all captives, including Nasser himself, and set them free to enable them return to Egypt. The order was to follow a vocal promise by each that they won't engage in military or any other hostile activity against the State of Israel once their freedom was granted.

Questioning the wisdom of such an order, reliable sources revealed that due to US pressure, threatening cuts in supplies, landing and docking privileges, we were forced to grant freedom to a major enemy officer like Gamal Abdul Nasser. The American idea behind it was that granting him freedom to return to Egypt will encourage him, and others, to change their attitudes towards Israel. Furthermore, three thousand enemy troops were granted freedom along with him. However, shortly after his release, Gamal Abdul Nasser became President of Egypt, increased hostilities against Israel ten fold, and vowed to crush the Zionist regime once and for all.

So much for promises.

Meanwhile, Nasser shook hands with Major Dayan when released. His smile was supposed to express friendship, and appreciation, although, in my opinion, his eyes expressed what he really felt: hatred, anger and hostility.

Though he didn't say so, I knew that Major Dayan wasn't pleased with the effect of that order. We all felt that releasing enemies for no reason was a waste of manpower, equipment, and limited resources. The price was heavy: many casualties our units suffered at the hands of Egyptian forces. In my opinion, as well as Major Dayan's belief, Israel should have done what's best for the security of the country, rather than shake in their boots and oblige every time U.S. naively pushed the Prime Minister to jeopardize Israel's basic security. Despite politics and pressures, the War of Liberation had to continue. The next offensive led our forces through the Negev and into the section of the Sinai Peninsula still under Egyptian control.

Since we advanced swiftly, crushing Egyptian resistance on the way, a request was forwarded to the Israeli Air-Force to go ahead and bombard the retreating Egyptian forces in advance of our final assault. Having problems with some of our military trucks, we used vehicles acquired from the retreating enemy forces. The enemy vehicles had Egyptian insignias and clear markings. Israeli flags on each vehicle was supposed to let people know that they now were under Israeli control.

Within hours we advanced all the way through Ujah-El-Haffir in the Sinai Peninsula, about fifty miles into Egyptian territory. That's when the Israeli Air Force completed the bombardments of other locations, and rushed to bombard Egyptian positions in Ujah-El-Haffir.

However, due to the fact that our communication equipment was old, and unreliable, the pilots didn't get the message that the positions were already under our control. In their zeal to soften the enemy when they spotted our vehicles with Egyptian insignias, they believed they were decimating the enemy. In effect our Air-Force bombarded the daylights of us, killing and injuring many in our units.

By the time our Air-Force became aware of the error, and left, our medics tried to save the lives of many in my unit. The casualties, result of friendly fire didn't stop regiment command from urging us to pursue the enemy and capture El-Arish before United Nations would declare another cease-fire that would further help the enemy.

Among the Israeli troops, the regiment had a special unit commanded by Yaaqov Garneck, the notorious Lehi member known as "the tall blond" whose expertise included robbing British Banks to finance underground activity. The captain was first to reach Ujah-El-Haffir. He had a bad habit of standing on the jeep driven by his designated driver, giving orders to his men. Despite warnings by his men that this practice exposed him to danger, he repeated the same when he reached town. Following a brief skirmish, the Egyptian forces, estimated at three or four regiments, raised a white flag, expressing their preference to surrender rather than die.

Captain Garneck, believing it was a legitimate wish to surrender, ordered the enemy to throw all guns and ammunition into one pile in the center of town. My doubts about surrendering all their weapons as instructed were fully justified. They always played tricks, and in my experience, they couldn't be trusted to keep their word.

Surprise: the enemy troops obeyed.

Captain Garneck ordered his men to collect the weapons, surround the prisoners and herd them in one area to be encircled by a barbed wire fence. While his orders were implemented, he stood tall on the jeep, ignoring the fact that his body was exposed to hostile elements.

Suddenly, a single shot whistled through from behind a pile of debris. The enemy sniper took upon himself to fire and shoot the naive captain. The bullet ripped Captain Garneck's neck beyond repair. He collapsed on the spot, his body rolled halfway out of the vehicle while blood oozed from the wound like from an open faucet.

His second in command, First Lieutenant Gaby, though angry and tense, continued with the operation according to the rules of engagement. He refrained from taking revenge despite his feelings about enemy's tactics.

Another shot whizzed by aimed to eliminate Gaby as well. This time the sniper's bullet missed, triggering a quick search. The sniper, realizing that his chances to escape diminished, aimed another bullet at the new company commander. This time he didn't miss: Gaby's right shoulder dripped blood almost at the same time his Sergeant responded with a burst of fire from his sub-machine-Gun. The sniper was hit, his chest riddled with bullets.

The strictly enforced curfew that followed discovered that several other enemy soldiers, not just the sniper, were still around, trying to take out the new company commander. They were promptly eliminated one by one until firing stopped altogether.

CHAPTER TWENTY TWO

United Nations Security Council declared, and enforced, another cease-fire. Israeli troops stopped their advance into Egyptian territory as instructed by David Ben-Gurion to obey the Security Council decision. It should be noted that during this war, almost in each battle, cease-fires were enforced when Israeli troops broke through enemy lines, advancing rapidly into the Egyptian mainland.

It seemed that United Nations never interfered when Israeli troops were overwhelmed, pulling back to reorganize, or in need of rest. For reasons unknown to me or fair-minded people, no cease-fire was declared, nor enforced, when the Arab armies advanced, period.

Despite the cease-fire, Israeli troops remained sitting in their positions, awaiting new orders from the Defense Minister, namely, David Ben-Gurion, whose policies were guided by what he termed "what will the world say?" In other words, world public opinion was a major component influencing his decisions. On the other hand, Menachem Begin advocated the opposite: if Israel's security interest demanded Israeli actions be subject to restrictions because of oil interests of U.S. and the Europeans, in his opinion, Israel's physical well being should have priority. Many politicians leaned towards Ben-Gurion's policies, only a few had the sensitivity to consider Israel's interests. A big number of countries, in Europe and elsewhere, were merely following their Anti-Semitic tendencies, regardless of obvious perils to Israel's existence.

While sitting in the trenches, Election Day came due in Israel to determine whether to have David Ben-Gurion continue as Prime Minister and Defense Minister, or have Menachem Begin, the opposition leader, take the reigns of government. Elections in Israel were always very noisy, tricky, allowing smears, and innuendos. Public opinion indicated a very close election ahead, and that's when the dirty schemes began. Being that labor was in power, they seemed to use their rule to influence the results.

Election laws were strictly enforced.

The law stated that no one can vote unless he has a valid Identification Card. Since Israeli troops didn't get yet such cards which were introduced while they were manning the frontlines, many in the military couldn't participate in the vote unless the cards reached them in time. The National Elections were two weeks away, yet no cards reached the division's troops.

Election Day arrived.

The entire division was still waiting for ID cards, unable to participate. It should be noted that the division numbered about 15,000 to 20,000 men, and it was well known that the majority would have voted for Menachem Begin due to the fact that most were members of Etzel and Lehi and many other supporters who appreciated his political agenda.

The tendency to control the elections in favor of the ruling party was definitely an illegal advantage for labor and the socialist lefties. Yet, no one but the local population, objected to such tactics. United States, of course, especially those who did everything to manipulate Israeli politics to agree with U.S. guidelines, found it easier to deal with David Ben-Gurion. They believed that he was more obliging when pressured than Menachem Begin, who was known by reputation as a stubborn nationalist.

While U.S. policy from the start strived to support a miniscule Israeli state in order to please the Arab oil producers, Begin was too strong a character to be pushed around. The same attitude by U.S. policy makers continued to this very day. The State Department was always guided by sympathy for the Arabs believing that the Arab oil would help keep U.S. prosperous and strong. The Arab oil, in fact, weakened U.S. considerably, depriving the biggest power in the world from being really independent, and do what's right and just regardless of material gains.

Despite predictions that Begin was destined to win the elections, Ben-Gurion won a landslide victory, if official records could be trusted. Still, no one can prove with certainty that he actually won the way officials insisted.

CHAPTER TWENTY THREE

The war was definitely over after Egypt, Jordan, and Syria were decisively defeated on the ground, the air and in all sea battles. The Arab armies that attacked full force, challenging tiny Israel, suffered heavy casualties in all clashes, mostly due to the fact that the Israeli army was, for the most part, Special Forces, similar to the British Commandos as well as Special Forces in the U.S. military.

The missions were big but the units defending or attacking enemy positions were small with limited supplies. They had to account for every bullet fired and any equipment lost or destroyed. Eventually, Egypt and Jordan signed a peace agreement with Israel. Since Syria lost the Golan Heights, they refused to negotiate a peace treaty unless the Golan will be returned to them without pre-conditions.

The Golan hills overlooked northern Israel for many years, causing havoc in the Israeli valley. From their high positions, the Syrians were in a habit to fire at Israeli farmers below, preventing planting and harvesting. They also caused unprovoked casualties among Israeli farmers, as well as the civilian population at large.

Returning that hilly land to Syria was out of the question.

The Syrian politicians insisted on getting the entire Golan back. Israel rejected their demand since the condition was intended to enable their sharp-shooters return to their destructive habit of sniping at Israeli citizens at will.

Since the war was over, the Israeli military discharged most personnel except officers and non-commissioned officers. Filing a request to be discharged as well to enable me pursue journalistic aspirations, my hopes were high. After all, I had a degree in Journalism and Creative Writing from a British College, but no desire to serve in the military longer than absolutely necessary. In my opinion, the longer I wait the more difficult it'd be to get a job in my favorite field.

My request was denied.

My appeal, the same day, was denied as well. I was informed that the denials originated directly from the Southern Command. The next day, after all my men were already home enjoying their civilian freedoms, my life was still subject to military discipline.

Distressed, my mood close to depression, convinced me that someone in authority had it in for me. Unexpectedly, a special messenger came to look for me. The message, in form of an order from higher ups, stated that General Itzchak Sadeh, the man in charge of the Southern Command, wanted me to report to him with no delay at fourteen hundred hours sharp.

Having the rest of the morning to worry about what the general wanted me for, probably added a few more white hair on top of my head. Despite my connections I failed to get an answer or even a guess to calm my nerves. That's the time when Prime Minister David Ben-Gurion, who was still Defense Minister, ordered that all military personnel must salute officers in military camps and jurisdictions.

Having no idea what the general had in store for me, I dressed up in proper military attire. Reaching the general's office at fourteen hundred hours as ordered ready for whatever will be will be, my hope was that if I'm properly dressed, and honor him with the first salute in our camp, he'll be more sympathetic to my plea to be discharged.

Stopping in front of his desk, the salute was impressive, "Reporting as ordered, general," I said.

Without looking up, he responded, "Stop that nonsense, soldier, just sit down." I knew for a long time, and he made no secret of it, that he was not a spit and shine general. He hated the salute orders as much as any other officer during that period.

Sitting down in front of his desk, sweating profusely, not knowing whether he was impressed, my voice slightly hoarse uttered, "General, sir, I think I'm entitled to an explanation."

He waved his hand, and said, "I'll be with you in a minute. Be patient, soldier, will you?"

The general was close to seventy five, his sideburns white and short while bald spots were showing here and there on top of his skull. The hair, for the most part, was still dark brown, almost chestnut in color. While he was looking at a bunch of typewritten papers, adjusting his reading glasses from time to time, I admired the man's physic which looked much younger than his real age. He was muscular, appeared to have self-control, and enough energy to compete with most young officers under his command.

Fifteen minutes later, he shoved the papers aside with a sigh. He asked, "You want a discharge, don't you, soldier?"

"Yes, general. My unit was discharged. How come I'm left behind – is this a punishment of some sort?"

The general forced a smile. "Sorry, but I can't let you go yet," he declared. "Subordinates are privates, you're an officer."

"Why am I excluded general? I met a bunch of officers who were discharged as well."

"We need you here for the time being. Why the objection, soldier – don't you like the army?"

He called everybody "soldier", no name or rank. It was an old habit of his, and habits were always hard to break.

"General, I like the army, sure, but I wouldn't make a career out of it – I'm a journalist by trade, sir, and would prefer…"

"Yes, I know."

"Then why am I still here, sir?"

He smiled. "I have a special mission for you, soldier. Please be patient." He leaned back on his seat, looked straight at me with enquiring eyes and reshuffled the printed papers on his desk.

Patient I was not. I couldn't tell him so for fear that I'd be scolded or maybe charged with something. "A mission?"

"Yes, you may call it that."

"The war is over, I think, general – what would the mission be?"

He ignored my question, asking instead, "D'you know Major Haran?"

"Yes, general – he's Education officer of the division."

"He recommended you for the mission."

Unable to ascertain the nature of the mission, I was at loss for words. "I'm sorry, general, I still don't know what is the mission – is it combat related?"

The general laughed. "No, it's about the creation of a Division Magazine I'm planning. Major Haran recommended you for editor."

Stunned, looking at him with disbelief, doubting whether my qualifications justified the recommendation, I made it clear to the general that I was never the editor of anything, except for a small circulation scandal sheet in my teens before I knew better.

"If that's an order, general, I'll try, but I can't give you any guaranty."

To my surprise, the general said, "It's not an order, soldier, it's a personal request."

"If I disagree, will it affect my discharge?"

"No, of course not."

Pausing several seconds, I said, "Fine, general, I'll try. Thank you for trusting me."

The general flipped through the papers on his desk, and gave me several pages. "Read this material and let me know what you think of it as an editor, please."

Glancing through the narrative, I realized that whoever wrote it knew a lot about military and political affairs. I said, "That's an excellent narrative, general – I don't see the name of the author, though – who wrote it?"

The general hesitated. Finally, he said, "I wrote it. Do you agree?"

Shocked to learn that the general dared criticize anything the Defense Minister supported, I said, "Yes, general, I agree to most of it."

The loud knock on the door startled me.

The general said, "This must be Major Haran – come on in, major!"

The major, a tall man with beach-blond hair, lean and muscular walked in briskly, stopped in front the desk, saluted, and said, "Major Haran reporting, general."

"Sit down, major," the general pointed to a chair next to mine. "Your recommendation is accepted," he said. "Now, you take it from here, major. Make all arrangements necessary and let's get moving, the sooner the better."

"Thanks, general, I appreciate your trust in my judgment."

"Here is my contribution, major," he handed him his own narrative, adding, "That's all for now. You know what has to be done. If you have any problem, let me know."

"Can we leave now, general?"

"Yes, of course – dismissed."

Major Haran looked at me, got up, saluted, urging me to do the same. Emulating his example, my salute was brisk while turning around, following him to the door. Once outside, Major

Haran stopped, handed the general's narrative over to me with a smile.

"Did you read this?" he asked.

"Yes, I read every word, major – why?"

"He may be right, but I disagree on one: saluting is a must in military environment in order to preserve discipline, right?"

"I agree with you, but…"

The major interrupted and said, "Let's leave the buts out for a while. First let's go to my office and discuss the magazine: budgets, the printing and the materials we are allowed to publish - are you with me?"

"Yes, major, I'm with you, just lead the way."

Once we settled down in his office, the major collected a bunch of papers on his desk and handed them over to me. "This is all the material our Division periodical received so far. Mostly officers journalistic efforts."

"Major, I can't include them all, only the best, no matter who wrote them, d'you agree?"

The major smiled, "Absolutely, you're the editor."

"Thanks, major - can I go now?"

"Not yet. The general asked me to try and convince you to sign up for the regular army – can you be convinced?"

"No, major, I'm not regular army material."

"Why not? The conditions are great: you'll get lodging free, a car and a driver at your disposal, free food and many other privileges."

"Except freedom."

"If you sign for twenty years, you'll be sent to a military Academy in England. On graduation the rank of Lieutenant Colonel will be bestowed upon you with all privileges – well, what d'you say?"

"No, I'm not a military man, major. Give up, please."

"The army needs young officers, I doubt they'll give up."

I wanted to say many things that I doubted the major would like but after a brief pause, realization hit me that antagonizing the major, and the general, wasn't a very good idea.

"What will happen if you tell the general I don't wish to sign? Would I be punished?"

"No, of course not," the major said, and looking away, he added, "but then all officers in the division will be discharged in a month or so, except you."

His prediction wasn't to my liking. "The army cannot keep me forever, can they?"

"You'll have to stick around at least six more months. You wouldn't like that, would you?"

This sounded to me like blackmail. "My civilian lawyer will sue, major. What then?"

"You'll lose, it's your word against the army's word."

"That's not fair at all."

"May I ask you why you'd refuse a high rank and a promising career?"

"I hate giving orders," I said. "Especially when danger is involved."

The major looked me over as though he never saw me before.

*   *

*

Since the cease-fire was in effect with no end in sight, Major Dayan authorized for me a leave of four days, provided Sergeant Benjamin took over temporarily.

Visiting my parents in Zikhron-Yaaqov, I enjoyed a few home cooked meals, plus a long rest with no worry about the destroyed zipper on the sleeping bag or sharing my bed with rattlesnakes.

Four days later, I was back in Sinai. The problem was that for the first time in the history of this desert rain clouds exploded above the camp area, soaking tents, and fabrics. That's about the time I reached my unit. While doing everything possible to arrive during daylight hours, I reached the camp area just as darkness set in.

Unable to see who was on guard, I advanced towards the guard's boot. A voice, loud enough to be heard, suddenly demanded, "Halt or I shoot!"

I recognized the sentry's voice. While giving him the password as required, I advanced casually ahead.

"Don't move!" the sentry yelled.

"David, I gave you the password, it's me, your company commander, don't you recognize me?"

"No," the sentry insisted. "Drop to the ground or I shoot!"

"Okay, David, I'm on the ground - what d'you want me to do?"

The sentry's voice sounded sarcastic, "C r a w l!"

"Are you crazy, David? Everything is wet here, and you know me."

The password was regularly changed every other day. David knew I couldn't have gotten the new password. He just enjoyed making me crawl. Apparently it was payback time for him. Two weeks ago, scolding him for smoking on guard, he was punished by having to dig ditches in the desert until his hands were covered with blisters.

The loud exchanges with the sentry brought Sergeant Benjamin on the double. "What's going on, David?"

"There's someone here who claims to be the company commander but he doesn't know the password. I can't see him and I don't know who he is."

Sergeant Benjamin raised his voice, "You idiot, it is the commander – let him in – I recognize his voice."

Forced to let me in, David didn't sound very happy. "If you say so, sergeant."

As I arrived, still wet from ground puddles, huffing and puffing, trying to shake off dirt, Sergeant Benjamin said, "David, you're excused pending trial. You knew who he is, dammit!"

"It's okay, sergeant. It's my fault. I should have known the password. He did what's right. I only hope he'll do the same if an enemy comes along."

"No trial, Commander?"

"Not this time."

CHAPTER TWENTY FOUR

Finally, the war was over not due to signed peace agreements, rather because the Arab armies were exhausted, demoralized and decided that they couldn't win. Most Arab states remained hostile, vowing to continue the fight in the future. Meanwhile, all Muslim states, including the Arab League, declared a boycott of Israeli products. They assumed that if they couldn't defeat Israel militarily, they'll achieve the same effect economically. However, the boycott was a joke: many merchants in Arab countries bought Israeli products, removed the stickers "Made in Israel", replaced them with theirs, and resold them to Muslim countries where they were gobbled up.

Moreover, many Arabs dignitaries arrived in Jerusalem for medical treatment, requesting not to stamp their passport with an Israeli stamp since they'll face punishment on their return home. Many of them, vocal against Israel, advocated in public against buying Israeli products, but they themselves gobbled up anything originating in Israel.

The interesting fact is that when American forces captured Baghdad and searched Sadam's warehouses, they found lots of Israeli Nesher beer, a drink known to contain alcohol. Alcohol was always prohibited by the Islamic religion, however, it was well known that Sadam's family was crazy about it.

No matter what, the boycott is still prevalent.

Except the regular army, most Israeli reservists were discharged to give veterans the opportunity to find available jobs. Discharged long after the war ended, my biggest problem wasn't getting a job, rather getting a loan to enable me buy clothes to dress appropriately.

All my clothes were devoured by a spreading fire through the barracks, including mine, a few days before my discharge. The only clothes available to me were the ones having on that day: one pair of short pants, one pair of shoes, one shirt and a pair of underwear.

Being told that there's an office helping veterans to re-enter civilian life, I went to ask for a small loan. Explaining what happened, clarifying that I had a job to go to, getting a loan shouldn't be a problem. A heavy set young man, sitting at a desk cluttered with papers, rudely asked, "So what d'you want us to do?"

Israelis were never known to be polite, no matter what was the nature of their job. That could be because the Hebrew language is straight and direct, rather than diplomatic.

"I was discharged from the service - all my clothes were destroyed in a fire."

"I repeat: so, what d'you want us to do?"

"I need a small loan to enable me buy clothes."

"You have a job?"

"Yes, of course."

"Why don't you ask your boss for an advance on your salary?"

"That'd be stupid. I was just hired."

"Are you a new immigrant?"

"No, what's that to do with it?"

"We only help new immigrants."

"What – what the hell are you saying?"

"I'm saying since you're not a new immigrant you have family and friends that can help you – ask them for money."

"You mean, veterans that were born or grew up in this country are not entitled to a loan?"

"Yes, that's exactly what I mean," he smiled, pointing to the line forming behind me. "Move," and raising his voice, he added, "next, please!"

Furious, though restrained, I said, "Thanks for nothing!"

Had I made excessive noise he could call the police and have me removed by force. On my first day out as a civilian I didn't feel like having the police handle me. Unable to go to work in an office with short pants and a soiled shirt, I asked a neighbor to let me borrow his for a day or until I'll be able to get money to buy some.

I realized that without party affiliation no one would help me get back on my feet. Not being a member of any party was a big problem during that period. The party provided connections, access to jobs and financial help. Being stubborn by nature, refusing to join a party I didn't agree with, and I didn't agree with most of them, didn't help me. Each party had some good ideas as well as bad ideas. If I could take the good ones only from each, the combined ideas would be more appealing.

The first civilian job was with the Postal Authorities which included the telephone department in Tel-Aviv. Passing a test resulted in getting grade C. The grades indicated the wage level. Grade A was the highest rank, and E being the lowest. Being a Grade C , the assignment was of a supervisory position in the Tel-Aviv main telephone exchange.

My job was to make sure that everything runs smoothly, and at the same time take care of complaints. On the first day, noticing that the room in which the main exchange was located was very crowded, bothered me. Employees were too crammed to be efficient. I put a note in the suggestion box for higher-ups to consider. Four days later passed, yet nothing happened. No one read the notes in the suggestion box, probably, since no one hinted that management will look into it.

Since my suggestion was ignored, I called for a general meeting of the employees whereas I explained that the working conditions are inadequate. I wasn't talking about wages, only about the crowded conditions.

The meeting agreed with a majority of hands that the management should be informed, as well as warned that unless the situation is corrected, we'll declare a strike for two hours. Management, once again, ignored our threat for a strike, the first ever in a government controlled section of operations.

Since management ignored the strike threat, we knew we had to do something. We decided to start the strike, after a long discussion, the next day from 10.00 AM to 12.00 noon. Management was promptly notified, and once again, the strike threat wasn't considered.

The next day, 10.00 AM sharp, as promised, all telephone circuits to and from Tel-Aviv came to a stop. Half an hour later the Postmaster General of Tel-Aviv paid a hurried visit to the main exchange, and asked to talk with the organizers of the strike.

The employees pointed to me.

Many of them feared that if they'll be associated with me they'll all be fired. Mr. Rohald, the Tel-Aviv Postmaster General, took me aside, and asked, "Why didn't you suggest to improve crowded conditions through the normal channels before declaring a strike in a government department which is prohibited by law?"

"I did but you ignored it!"

"When was that?"

"Would that make a difference?"

"Depending on your suggestion."

"The suggestion was clear – you ignored it completely."

"What you did is illegal."

Smiling, although I felt that he had the power to fire me as well, I said, "Sir, we suggested several times and put our written requests in the suggestion box but no one responded – not you or anyone else."

"No such suggestion reached me," he said.

"Hard to believe, sir. I have copies of the suggestions if you care to read them – would you like to see them now, sir?"

He pulled a piece of paper from his pocket, glanced at it, and stated, "You started your job only a week ago – no one before you complained, why is that?"

I could tell that he was angry, and more than that, he tried to blame me entirely for incitement of government employees. In other words, he felt that I was a trouble-maker and should watch my step.

"I don't know why, sir. Ask my predecessors, please," I said, "but when I see something wrong, no matter where, I fight to correct it."

He hesitated for a minute or so. Taking in the room, the sitting positions, and the limited space, he said, "Fine, I understand the problem. I have to think about it, and see what I can do – in the meantime, I'd appreciate if you'll convince your colleagues to go back to work – is that a deal?"

Scratching my head, I wet my lips, shook his extended hand, and said, "We'll end the strike right now, but if no concrete response reaches us, we'll wait until the day after tomorrow at noontime."

"You'll have an answer by then, I'm sure."

"If we have no positive answer, we'll strike again – is that a deal?"

"Yes," he agreed, turned around and left.

Employees who listened to the conversation cheered, and encouraged all others to resume work. They considered me a hero, but many said they thought they may still be fired as a result. The next day arrived and none of us were fired yet. In the afternoon, about 3.00 PM, management notified me that I was promoted to grade B, and transferred to work as a cashier in the central Post Office.

No explanation was given.

Suspecting that my promotion was an attempt to bribe me to ignore the employees strike threat, I was ready to continue with the fight – would the employees be ready to follow me? Mr. Rohald, figuring since I wasn't with them any longer, no one would continue, perhaps even cancel the strike threat.

It was obvious to me that the Postmaster didn't like me, especially my rebellious-critical tendencies. To be on the safe side, before I'll be stuck in a no-advance position, I submitted many articles to various newspapers to advance my journalistic aspirations. My articles were published, including several special investigative reports. That's when I spotted an ad in the morning papers that United Press was looking for a news editor in the Tel-Aviv branch.

Meanwhile, Tel-Aviv Postmaster transferred me again, this time from the Main Post Office to a small branch in the north, assigned to work as a cashier. Just as I reached the northern branch, a message reached me that United Press chief was willing to interview me for the news editor job.

While waiting for a response from the United Press Chief, a publisher approached me to translate a series of suspense novels from English into Hebrew. Due to the number of novels to translate, over one hundred, my time was very limited. I tendered my resignation to the Postmaster General. It seemed to me he was happy to get rid of an internal critic, or trouble-maker as he apparently called me.

Two weeks thereafter, following the interview by United Press Chief, I was hired on the spot. My work entailed reading 20,000 words every evening, re-writing and editing news items received by code and printed on hard copy from all over the globe. The edited news were submitted to local Hebrew newspaper subscribers concentrated in Tel-Aviv area. The work kept me busy every night from the evening hours through several hours after midnight.

While word got out about my editing job with United Press, a known religious newspaper representative approached me, offering a daily writing job to write their editorials using various pen names enabling them to use as their own. Since the pay promised was adequate, I gave it a try, writing editorial opinions on various topics. The subjects included military, economy, political and world affairs. Since the editorials carried pen names no one could associate them to me.

It felt strange to read in the morning my editorial opinions in the name of the newspaper. The first week I received a substantial amount of Israeli Pounds for my efforts. The second week, I received only partial payment with the excuse that they were temporarily short of funds. As the weeks went by my monetary income shrunk. Several months later, realizing that the newspaper owed me an accumulated figure of several thousand Israeli Pounds, justified by the same lame excuse of being short of cash funds, my worry was that my pay will never materialize.

Asking for the money was like talking to the wall: each time the excuses grew more colorful, and there seemed to be no end in sight. Finally, I informed them that unless payment is forthcoming, I'll stop writing their editorials.

Since that didn't help, I contacted Buchalter, my attorney. After detailed explanations, my lawyer said that the only way to collect was to file a lawsuit. Buchalter was right, since despite my repeated calls to the newspaper owners, and several messages left for them, no one responded.

My lawyer secured a court date, and informed me that I didn't have to be present, only if I wanted to. Curious about his handling of such a case, I went to court on the designated date and watched the proceedings. Buchalter was a brilliant attorney; and when he spoke, he sounded like a live encyclopedia. When he explained to the judge he quoted laws on the books and precedents no one seemed to remember. He mentioned laws and sentences rendered in many cases of similar nature with such accuracy that the judge was impressed and overwhelmed. Within twenty minutes, the defendants were ordered to pay-up with interest, including court costs. The defendant's representative requested an extension stating his client had cash flow problems. The client, he stated, just deposited a big check in the newspaper's account, expecting it to clear within three days.

The judge was reluctant to accept postponement of the payment. He said, "Very well. The defendant has four days to pay.

If by the fourth day the debt isn't cleared, a fine will be added at the amount of an additional one thousand pounds, is that clear?"

The attorney for the defense looked pathetically restrained as he meekly said, "Yes, your honor."

On the fourth day a certified check was delivered by special messenger to my attorney's office, including court costs, interest and attorney fees.

CHAPTER TWENTY FIVE

With the financial situation solved, my lucky streak seemed to continue when Yedioth Achronot, a mass circulation evening newspaper, accepted my articles and reports on a regular basis, including handling special investigative reports.

In a string of special reports, the first was depicting diamond smuggling inside salami products destined for the USA by a bunch of corrupted young rabbis. Next was an investigative report detailing a well organized smuggling ring involving drugs, and illegal money transfers. Several additional reports followed, adding shining examples to my credit.

My lucky streak evaporated, however, when David Ben-Gurion, the first Prime Minister of Israel, showed his true colors as a politician by appointing his own son, Amos Ben-Gurion, as Chief of Tel-Aviv Police, the most populated city in Israel. I decided to look into it, and what I discovered rattled my confidence in politics and politicians.

In the first place, in my opinion, a Police Chief should be a person with know-how, honesty and experience. Amos Ben-Gurion, on the other hand, represented the opposite: he was a known drunk, married a drunk English woman, using abusive language to express himself in public against anyone who happened to be in the way.

Information about the new Police Chief was made available to me by many witnesses who stated that he was a drunk before his appointment. Habits were hard to break, so he continued with his drunken behavior to the point that even when he was in full police uniform showing his high rank, he was still the same obnoxious, arrogant person. The appointment didn't change his attitude, and definitely, not his character.

Having no idea whether his father, the Prime Minister who appointed him, knew about his indiscretions, I began to collect notarized witnesses statements, photos proving my assertions, as well as reports in words and photos of pushing and spitting on citizens to move out of his way.

The folder was already fifty pages long when witnesses revealed he took bribes to approve confirmations of good character. Such confirmation was needed to enable job hunting, applying for foreign currency allocations etc. Press photographers supplied me with photographic evidence as well as their notarized testimony.

Being convinced that his father wasn't aware of the situation, I tried to get an appointment to present the folder. My intention was to warn him that this disgrace cannot continue.

The Prime minister's frequent speeches about honesty, character and sacrifice for the good of all, were well known. However, I knew better: as a youngster he was arrested several times for various reasons. When he joined the British military he was accused many times of desertion, as well as avoiding duties.

Political cronies labeled the Prime Minister as a statesman of stature, among other qualities which he never had, succeeded worldwide to convince foreign politicians that he was what they said he was.

The facts didn't portray him that way.

World supporters believed that David Ben-Gurion was the one to initiate and declare Israel as an independent democracy. **He was not.** The historical fact was that he was pressured by Etzel and Lehi.. In order to avoid being left behind, he declared independence. If Begin (Etzel leader) and Yellin (Lehi leader) didn't push him, he and his supporters might be still hiding under the bed, fearing what the British would do, as well as what the rest of the world would say about the "chutzpa" (nerve in Hebrew) to declare independence.

Ben-Gurion's supporters would probably attempt to rebuff such conclusions, believing that a lie repeated a thousand times would at the end be considered the truth. Propaganda was an effective tool in labor's political persuasions. The labor movement at that time used that tool to advance their agenda. Even the most effective individual equipped with a high IQ, character, honesty, and leadership abilities, if he didn't believe in the labor's philosophy, he was labeled ignorant and stupid. At the end, following repetitions, he would be considered as such.

Nowadays, the Palestinians in their quest to defeat Israel, use the same system against the Israeli Government. They repeat that Israeli troops committed atrocities, and show fake photos on TV day after day. They repeated the same so many times that the world believes that to be the truth. Example: the proclaimed

Jeninn massacre that **never was**. A long period after, it was proven to be a fabricated vicious Palestinian lie.

Despite labor's habits, I gave the Prime Minister the benefit of the doubt when a definite appointment was made to see him in his office. I took the thick folder with me figuring that when he'll see the evidence against Amos with his own eyes, he will agree to correct the wrong and remove him from public office.

CHAPTER TWENTY SIX

Security in and around Ben-Gurion's office was very tight. Even a tiny fly would have a hard time sneaking in. Carrying the heavy folder with me, I approached his office, and stopped when the military police ordered me to show my ID. Putting the folder on the floor, took my wallet out, flipped through it until I found the ID, and presented it to the Military Police officer. He looked it over from all angles, checked to see if my name is on the list, knocked on the door, and when instructed to let me in, I picked up the folder from the floor and entered.

David Ben-Gurion was seated by a long mahogany desk full of papers. He didn't lift his head to see who came in. This gesture apparently was supposed to inform me that the interview wasn't important to him. I cleared my throat twice to get his attention, but he wouldn't respond to that either. Two minutes elapsed before he raised his eyes, looked me over carefully, probably wondering about the content of the thick folder in my hands.

"Yes, I remember now: you represent Yedioth Achronoth. Sit down."

Sitting slow and easy, I had a chance to examine the wild brown-gray hair decorating his skull. To get his attention, I cleared my throat for the third time.

"May I ask," he said bluntly, "what's the purpose of your visit?"

"I'm here to bring to your attention that the appointment of your son in the capacity of Tel-Aviv Police Chief is wrong."

His face tightening, his brown eyes hardened when he said, "Oh, I see."

To prevent him from dismissing my declaration before examining the evidence, I said, "This folder, sir, has all the details, if you care to look."

He took the folder off my hands and opened it on the desk. Flipping through the pages without reading anything, he glanced at the photos accompanying the narratives, straightened up in his easy-chair, and looked me over from top to bottom.

"This is a well constructed conspiracy," he said. "I know what you are trying to do – discredit me and the Government of Israel!"

"Sir, if you'll only read the evidence, you'll realize that these are facts based on the truth."

In order to stress how angry he was, he ripped pages from the folder, shredded them with his hands to pieces and called me names he always reserved for his bitter enemies. He did the same with the photos and threw the empty folder towards me. The empty folder landed in my lap.

"Sorry to disappoint you, sir," my voice was restrained, but very loud, "destroying the pages and photos won't change the facts: I have the originals – you destroyed only the copies."

The Prime Minister stood up, and raising his voice, he said, "You are a liar, your reports are all lies and the photos fabricated – you are nothing but a traitor!"

"But, sir, the materials you destroyed will be published - I thought you'll be reasonable so that I won't have to do that."

Raging, his lips tightening, he called the Military Police and ordered the officers to throw me out physically, never allow me or the paper I represent to come to his office or interview him or his staff ever again.

The officers grabbed my arms, and pushed me out of the office without saying a word. During that period the Government Press Division had a military censor going over each report before published, crossing out entire sections deemed dangerous to state security, officials, cabinet ministers as well as members of their families.

Accusing me of treason was bad enough, but what happened a day later was a lot worse. At three in the morning, someone knocked on my door vigorously, leading me to believe that there's a fire in the building. When I opened the door, a man in civilian clothes handed me a written message issued by military intelligence ordering me to be in Hakirya, the intelligence office, at 9.00 am sharp, to be interviewed by some major whose name wasn't mentioned, only that he is in charge of investigation of enemy agents. Before I could ask any questions as to the purpose of this, the man vanished.

Having no idea why I'd be summoned that way, I thought maybe the military wanted to convince me again to sign for the regular army, and attend a military academy in England like they did when I was still on active duty. There could be no other reason, I felt, since I did nothing wrong. If it was something to do with the reports I've written, the censor eliminated enough sections before approving my reports for publication, anyway.

The next day, 8.55 AM, I reported to the intelligence office in Hakirya, and showed them the note I received. No one informed me the name of the major in charge I was suppose to see. I was told to wait in the lobby until called.

The idea of sitting and waiting wasn't to my liking, since I had an assignment for the newspaper to take care of. Having no choice, I waited, looking at my watch every five minutes or so. Despite the message to report at nine o'clock sharp, my name wasn't called until 9.50AM. I was instructed to go to room number six and someone will come to see me soon. Again, I waited additional twenty five minutes when the door opened and a major in uniform, with no hat, strode in.

"We've a report you may be involved with enemy agents," he said. "D'you have any explanation?"

"First of all, major, I don't know who you are."

"I represent the Intelligence Service, Mister. My name isn't significant. Please explain your behavior."

"Behavior of what – what are you accusing me of?"

"We don't accuse you of anything yet," he spoke so fast I could hardly grasp the meaning of the words. "I have a report here that you intimidated the Prime Minister of the state – why is that?"

"That's the accusation?"

"Yes. Moreover, since you were a member of Lehi, we want to know the reason."

Smiling, I said, "I'm now a newspaper reporter, major, no longer an active member of Lehi, I went to the Prime Minister office after he granted me an interview with reference to the appointment of his son, Amos Ben-Gurion, as Tel-Aviv Police Chief."

"I see," he bit his lower lip, adding, "D'you know any enemy agents?"

"None whatsoever."

"Perhaps in the pursuit of information you stumbled into one without reporting the incident?"

"No, major, the entire assumption is ridiculous, and nothing like that ever happened."

The phone gave a shrill ring. The major picked up the receiver and said, "Yes, I understand, of course," and returned the phone to its cradle.

Having no idea who called the major and what was discussed, I couldn't tell whether he talked about me or not. I watched the major looking vacantly ahead, scratched his head and turned to face me. "Thank you for coming, Mister, that's all."

"You mean I'm free to go?"

"Yes, you may go," he said. "I'll personally look into your activity. If anything comes up, we'll let you know. Thank you for your cooperation."

And with that, he turned, opened the door, leaving in a hurry. The episode was very strange, unless the Security Service wanted to scare me into silence. If so, why didn't they accuse me of something, or detain me for further interrogation? Furthermore, it's strange that the major didn't reveal his name, and I had really no proof that this investigation ever occurred. The only reason could be perhaps they believed that my attorney could raise hell, perhaps make a big deal out of it. And that, politically speaking, won't look so good in the world press.

Once I left the intelligence office I didn't look back but I had a feeling I was being shadowed. To be sure, I signaled a cab and gave him an address to go to, not my own, or the newspaper I worked for. Looking back I spotted a cab behind us following closely. The moment I reached the central bus station in southern Tel-Aviv, I paid the cab and walked into the first building I reached. I spotted the cab stop as well, and a man in civilian clothes got off. He looked around him, trying to figure out where I went. Sticking close to the wall enabling me to see how frantic he became when he finally realized that he lost my trail.

Walking to the next street, I flagged another cab.

Certain that my shadow lost me, I gave the cabbie my private address. From home, I decided, I'd call my editor and explain what happened to me. As I opened the door into my first floor apartment, I spotted the man get off a cab. He seemed at loss as he scanned the immediate area, in particular the building I entered. To avoid being spotted, I rushed into the apartment, waited a while, opened the door and looked again: the man was nowhere is sight.

CHAPTER TWENTY SEVEN

Several days following the major's interrogation, the front pages of most Hebrew Daily newspapers were filled with details about Tamir, a young attorney, who filed suit against the Prime Minister, questioning his judgment by appointing his drunk son to such an important job. The suit claimed that Amos Ben-Gurion wasn't suitable to be Police Chief due to lack of qualifications and experience, as well as being drunk, and a shady character who took bribes for granting favors.

Attorney Tamir maintained that the appointed Police Chief's behavior, was documented with photos, plus notarized sworn statements from witnesses willing to come to court to testify before a judge. Some of the Dailies printed photos depicting the Police Chief behaving like a common criminal, as well as a drunk.

Tamir, unknown until that day became a celebrity admired by supporters and hated by opponents, probably members of the ruling party who voted the party line no matter what the problem. I did my best to tell the readers about my attempt to have the Prime Minister rescind the appointment. However, despite the solid facts, the military censor crossed out everything except my name which would present everything as irrelevant.

Frustration among journalists grew to anger, but the censor always had the last word, whether justified or not. The military censor was supposed to forbid disclosure of facts that may or may not cause damage to the state. In my opinion, accusing Amos of being a criminal had nothing to do with state security.

Since my attempts to inform the public failed, I tried to meet Tamir. Together, maybe, we can figure what to do legally to affect the outcome. Following all leads, including knocking on Tamir's apartment door, brought no results. Neighbors stated that they saw him pack and leave in a hurry.

Many said he looked scared.

Being unable to locate the daring lawyer led me to believe that threats may have been the reason. And when it involved politics, anything was possible, even beyond threats on his life. The Secret Service had the power to make his life miserable, like they tried with me. I wouldn't be surprised if they did just that, perhaps even more.

The Court date was two months ahead. I made a note of it, clearing my calendar to be present at the trial. Since this was an important case, a panel of three judges would decide the next step. The justice department was independent, I was told, so that the chances were the judgment would not be influenced by politics. Since Israel was blessed with thirty seven political parties, avoiding political influence wasn't easy.

The left had several parties in their corner, the right had many others, and the small religious parties had about a dozen or so. In the past the biggest party was called to form a coalition to govern. Each party strived to get more seats in the government so that they may be a decisive factor in all walks of life.

Two months wait was a long time since many other events could get more attention, and public interest may decline. Finally, the date arrived and I attended the court session. Tamir was there presenting his case, the defense attorneys presented their defense citing the law that the Prime Minister has a right to appoint anyone he trusts to such an important role.

Next to Tamir I saw several muscular young men, which I took to be body-guards. Having no idea whether they were armed, I assumed that they were at least experienced in martial arts and capable to perform their job.

The judges listened attentively to both sides.

An hour later, the panel asked if both sides are ready to present witnesses. Tamir answered in the affirmative. The defense attorneys requested a postponement to collect evidence, and bring in witnesses they maintained were difficult to locate.

I had no idea what could a postponement do for the state. Two months were enough, but the panel of judges, following a brief deliberation, decided to grant the state one more month to prepare.

As soon as the panel's decision was announced several muscular men whisked Tamir out of the courtroom. Trying to catch him and arrange a meeting between us was impossible. I noticed the young men shielding him. They helped him get into a four door sedan, closed the door fast, and before I could reach them, the vehicle roared and drove away.

Fearing there was a good reason for Tamir's security team, I imagined his life was threatened. It could be a political stunt designed to scare and force him to drop his lawsuit.

Scarring tactics weren't foreign to the labor movement.

For example, such tactic hit me in the past, when the phone rang in my apartment at three after midnight. Sleepily I picked up the phone and muttered, "Hello, who is it, please?"

The caller, a thick masculine voice, asked if it's me in person.

"Yes, but whatever it is can it wait until morning?"

"No, this is urgent," the man said. "I'm from the telephone department."

"Call me in the morning, please."

"This can't wait," he warned, "your life may be in danger."

"Okay, so what d'you want me to do?"

"Please do me a favor: measure the length of the phone line and let me know right away."

Sleepily, my mind still foggy, I said, "About six feet, I think."

"Very well, then," the thick voice said. "The line is long enough."

"Long enough for what?"

"Long enough to hang yourself, stupid!" his voice turned louder. I heard a sharp click before the line went dead.

Similar gimmicks were prevalently used to antagonize and irritate political rivals. I wasn't sure whether such behavior was authorized, but it could be that loyal idiotic party members believed its fun.

That was the last time I saw Tamir in public.

A month went by, the court case was on but Tamir didn't show up, and no one seemed to know where he was. Rumor stated that he was killed or severely injured in an accident. My own investigation showed no accident involving Tamir. No news item appeared about his demise. The police had no information as to his whereabouts either. No one else took over the case, and the panel of judges dismissed it altogether.

Tamir disappearance is still a mystery.

CHAPTER TWENTY EIGHT

Tamir episode faded with time.

Despite investigations by sympathizers, nobody could determine or guess what happened to him. While scanning newspapers and magazines, I spotted one that offered me the chance of a lifetime: the Voice of Israel Radio Broadcasting Service was looking for a news editor to replace the present editor who resigned due to health reasons.

The Voice of Israel Radio was supported and financed by the government, and I assumed that no political influences dominated their hiring policies. Anxious not to miss that opportunity, I picked up the phone, dialed the number printed in the morning paper, anxious to find out qualifications and requirements needed for that job.

A definite appointment was made with the station manager for nine o'clock AM the next day. Since the office opened daily at nine o'clock, I believed I'll be the first to be interviewed.

On arrival at nine o'clock AM sharp I was told to sit in the lobby until called because the manager was already busy with other applicants. Twenty five minutes later I was told to come in and enter the room on the left. By then doubts troubled me. Several applicants saw the manager ahead of me, and chances were that he already chose a candidate. The doubt increased when forty two minutes elapsed and I was still waiting.

Eight minutes later I was asked to go the manager's office on my right. The manager, sitting by a metal desk looked me straight in the eye and said softly, "Please sit down."

I sat across from him and asked, "Is the job still open, sir?"

The man, broad shouldered, clean shaven with curly blond hair, smiled wide and said, "Yes, the job is still open – we choose only the best taking into account qualifications and experience."

"Then I still may have a chance?"

"Yes, you do - what d'you think qualifies you for the job?"

"I have a degree in Journalism and many years experience with news editing." I gave him written documents as proof.

The manager smiled, looked the documents over and declared, "I'm impressed. If I decide to hire you when can you start to work?"

"In a week or so."

"I need a commitment earlier than that. How is in three days?"

"You mean Monday?"

"Yes, that's fine – so far you're the best candidate I've seen."

Surprised by his candor, I felt awkward. Even if that's how he felt, he shouldn't have revealed that to me. Other employers never bestowed such honor on a candidate. Many a time I heard the saying that praises will give a candidate "a swollen head."

I forced a smile. "Sir, I'm honored that you've chosen me, but you failed to mention wages, working conditions and benefits."

He handed me a booklet outlining just what I asked for.

Glancing through the booklet I decided to accept the offer. I filled a form he laid on the desk before me with my name, address and phone number and thanked him for choosing me.

"Congratulations," he said. "The Job is yours. See you in three days, eight o'clock."

We shook hands, I got up and walked towards the door.

Three days later, at 8.00 AM sharp I reported to the Radio Station. The receptionist asked for the purpose of my visit. "I'm the new news editor," I said.

Her brown eyes looked me over as she said, "No sir, I don't think so – we have a news editor as of yesterday – you must be mistaken."

When I raised my voice demanding to see the Station Manager, a man came out from the adjacent room. He turned to me and said, "I'm the assistant manager – what's the problem?"

I gave him all the details about the interview and the decision of the manager asking me to report at 8.00 AM. He looked very sympathetic but stated that he didn't understand how could that be since the manager hired someone else for that job.

"I'm sorry," he said. "You probably didn't understand."

I didn't like his answers, so I raised my voice to make sure that unless I get more believable explanations, I won't move until I see the manager to clarify the matter.

"If you don't calm down and leave right now, sir, I'll have the police handle it."

Being upset, but realistic as well, I left the premises and called Nathan Yellin More, Lehi's chief, asking for his assistance. That's when reality hit me: he said that he had similar complaints by other members of Lehi. The only explanation, in his opinion, was that the ruling party didn't trust members of the Lehi or Etzel underground movements, and feared that if we had a say, especially on the radio, the propaganda we may advance might enable us to gain power, perhaps even take over the government.

It hurt to know that underground members who sacrificed most of their life for the establishment of the state were subject to discrimination. That's when I realized that the state didn't want any Lehi and Etzel members around.

Since I met personally the leader of the labor movement, namely David Ben-Gurion, I knew for a fact that he hated anyone who disagreed with him. He was always surrounded for the most part with "yes men and women". Whoever dared criticize him for political or social reasons was considered an enemy. Yet, he appointed his crooked son to a high police position along with many of his friends, but rejected more qualified people who disagreed with him on other matters of policy.

CHAPTER TWENTY NINE

The Israeli Defense Forces reorganization changed from regular army to a military consisting mostly of veteran reserves to be called in time of strife. The regular armed forces consisted of a skeleton of veterans who were the basis of the military, and new recruits, male and female.

Males, eighteen and over, were required to serve three years and females, married with no children, a period of two years and six months. During the period of indoctrination the recruits went through basic training at first to be followed by vigorous specific advanced training for the branch of service assigned to.

The reservists, commissioned, non-commissioned officers as well as privates, were required to serve. Officers had to serve forty five days a year, others, including privates, only thirty days. That's about the time that I was told to report to military headquarters and meet some generals of the regular army for consultation.

Having no idea why I was singled out to confer with the generals, I suspected they found out something to blame me for. I feared it's another gimmick by labor to intimidate opponents. Remembering the phone call past midnight, the order to report to intelligence for investigation and Tamir's disappearance, gave me food for worry.

Reporting to military headquarters, I was led to an empty room, and instructed to wait. "Hurry up and wait" was always a tactic of intimidation or so I thought. This time, I didn't wait too long: ten minutes later two generals strode in, a wide smile pasted on their lips, and like in a rehearsed play, they both greeted me and sat down. One was a full general, the second was only a Lieutenant general. Their names didn't mean a thing to me since I never heard of them before.

I was so upset to be called and forced to obey whenever they felt like, that I dared ask, "I'd like an explanation why you singled me out to come and see you – did I do anything wrong?"

The general, blurting his name, which I forgot shortly after, smiled and said, "Nothing wrong. This is an unofficial meeting."

The Lieutenant general didn't smile. His dark brown eyes examined my face. "We read your service record with interest," he said, "especially your handling of a combat unit during the war. To the point: the military needs young officers to serve in the regular army. We felt you may consider joining us to serve the country."

I wasn't stunned this time, not even surprised, and even suspected that it might be a move to get rid of my criticism as a civilian. As a member of the armed forces I'd be prohibited from criticizing the army as well as the government.

Repeating the same as I explained to the efforts to enlist me while I was in active service, I said, "I'm a journalist, gentlemen. I like my occupation and won't give it up."

The general hastened to say, "If you sign for twenty years you have a chance to become a regular army general."

"I've been offered the same before," I said. "I'm not a military man. I don't like orders, either to give or receive. Sorry, but you're wasting your time as well as my time – I'm not interested, and no matter what, you can't force me to join."

The Lieutenant General cleared his throat. He asked, "In other words, you don't want to serve your country in time of need, is that it?"

This, I felt, was an insult.

"In time of need I served before and will serve again when necessary. However, I won't sign for twenty years no matter what you offer."

The general's facial expression soured.

"Is that your last word?"

"Yes."

The Lieutenant General was about to say something but checked himself. Without saying a word, they turned and walked out. They didn't indicate whether I was free to leave or continue to wait.

Fifteen minutes later, since no one told me otherwise, I left the room and stopped at the reception window. The receptionist informed me that the interview was over.

Since my refusal was definite, no one bothered me for a few weeks. However, being an officer on reserve, I was called to serve the yearly forty five days at the end of the year and another forty five days at the beginning of the next year – a total of ninety days.

Ninety days out of civilian circulation would put me in danger of losing my job. I had to hire others to fill in for me the obligations I had. The costs were very high since no one wanted to work for less.

The pressure to change my mind included stationing me in the South, the closest point to Egyptian territory from where I could watch, using the binoculars, movements in the Sinai desert. The post I was assigned to wasn't essential to the security of the state. I had no men under my command, I had to contact with other units and no telephone so that I may get in touch with my journalistic contacts.

During most of the ninety days reserve service I kept busy watching camels treading around, but nothing else. Being so bored, I busied myself stuffing colored sands into small bottles. I tried to contact the newspaper I worked for but my phone connection was interrupted so many times I had to give up and return to bottle stuffing.

As soon as my time was up, I rushed back to civilian life. I planned to write several articles about wasting time and energy of reserve personnel. The planned articles would have been long enough to explain the problem and my suggested solutions, but the military censor chopped most of it. The censor erased so many parts in the first article that forced me to demand explanations. The censor reasoning was that I gave the enemy essential data, thus endangering the security of the state. It made no sense to print the article with most major parts obliterated.

Forced to reconsider, I concentrated on other subjects of interest reference to the same like the meager pay of reservists during their yearly reserve duties. True, employers swallowed the losses in manpower for the first few weeks, but if it lasted longer, the burden shifted to the reservists themselves. That created difficulties, mostly damaging the economic well being of the families who worked for a living.

The military censor found my explanations and criticism helping the enemy as well. Most of the important points raised were erased and I was left with my name and several paragraphs only. If that was part of the pressure to force me join the regular army, it'll fail again. The more pressure I felt the more stubborn I became.

CHAPTER THIRTY

Despite several successive wars due to Arab provocations, Israel survived. Wounded many times, sometimes severely, Israel managed to recover. After each war, tiny Israel became bigger and stronger than before.

Egypt's assault on Yom Kippur, the Holiest Holiday in Judaism, was designed to surprise the Israeli army and take over the one hundred mile-long defense line protected only by several hundred soldiers. On Yom Kippur most Israeli service personnel were off. The Prime Minister at the time was Golda Meir. General Dayan was Defense Minister. They were all taken completely by surprise.

Although heavily outnumbered, the IDF repulsed the massive Egyptian offensive. Despite the fact that Israel had only minimal forces, the troops held on several days until the reserves were fully mobilized. The reserves, in support of the regulars, pushed back Egyptian attempts to cut through the Israeli lines. Among the units squashing the Egyptians, was Ariel Sharon's division. General Sharon broke through the Egyptian lines, crossed all barriers and encircled the Egyptian Third army, the biggest and best of Egypt's military forces.

Sharon's division prevented the Egyptian forces from leaving, thus forcing them to surrender, or be annihilated. The Egyptians, supported by the Soviet Union, were anxious to establish a foothold in the Middle East. They provided the Egyptian armed forces with the latest hi-tech radar to be used against the Israeli Air-force, hoping to dispel Israel's military superiority, thus gain the sympathy of the vast Islamic World.

The Soviet Union wasn't worried about the surrender of the Egyptian Third Army, however, they were vehemently opposed to Israel taking over the newest radar station they equipped the Egyptians with. They realized that if the radar will be in Israeli hands, thus enabling Western countries to examine it. They threatened Israel and indirectly the USA that they are going to allow Russian volunteers to help the Egyptian troops to drive Israel out. The threat wasn't appreciated by US President Richard

Nixon who ordered Four full divisions of Marines dispatched to the Middle East just in case.

The unwavering American response cooled off the Soviets instantly. They decided to threaten Israel with dispatching Russian pilots to protect the Egyptians instead. To that, Abba Even, the Israeli Ambassador to the United Nations said, "Let them come - we'll shoot them down as well."

The Egyptian air-force, when encountering the Israeli air-force suffered heavy casualties. So many Egyptian pilots were shot down, that the remaining ones refused to fly to confront the Israelis. Russian pilots, in order to encourage the Egyptians, vowed to show them that the Israeli air-force can be defeated easily.

Two Egyptian jets piloted by Russians were shot down several days later. Despite the Egyptian uniforms, the pilots spoke no Arabic. That's when foreign press reporters realized they weren't Egyptians at all. They were interrogated by Russian speaking Israelis and their identities were confirmed.

When the pilots admitted their identities, their first request was political asylum. In consultation with Western powers, the British offered them shelter. It was known that should they be returned to Russia their lives would be in danger.

CHAPTER THIRTY ONE

Since that time, under extreme pressure from the United States, U.S secretary of state, Henry Kissinger, succeeded to convince the Egyptian Government to make peace with Israel for a price: Israel was forced to return to Egyptian control the oil fields their experts developed in the Sinai desert, as well as letting them have the entire peninsula. On top of all this, U.S. promised Egypt three billion dollars annual economic aid yearly as a bribe to encourage peace.

This wasn't a real peace,

It still isn't.

Despite promises, Egyptian officials did everything they could to distance themselves from establishing economic ties with Israel, which was normal development between countries at peace. Furthermore, every time hostile Arab elements killed or attacked Israeli civilians, Egyptian authorities justified them one hundred per cent, citing all kinds of excuses.

Following the Egyptian peace model, Jordan made a similar peace. They were attracted by similar financial aid from United States. Jordan, even nowadays, justifies most Hamas hostilities against Israel. The latest is Jordan's support for Saudi Arabia peace plan which demands that Israel return to 1967 ceasefire borders. However, these borders were the reason of continuous attacks by states like Syria from the Golan Heights, and Lebanon in the south. Israel was urged by most nations to give back to the Palestinian land essential to its security. Syria demanded the entire Golan back which they claim as Syrian territory. How can they demand the land carrying a Hebrew name, which was always part of Israeli land, is beyond any fair minded people.

The Palestinians demanded their own state. When the U.N. partition plan offered them a state, they refused to consider it. **They wanted all or nothing.** Since most Palestinians are raised with hatred against Jews and Israel, evident in their public school books, the chances for a settlement that will satisfy the security of Israel, is non-existent.

Let's be frank: the Arabs strive to chop Israel's territory and render it defenseless. The smaller Israel becomes, the more vulnerable it will be. No matter what they call it. No matter what falsehoods fabricated or propaganda lies were used, the truth proved them wrong. They labeled the Israelis Nazis, accusing them for killing their children. The truth shows that those were the children they trained and sent into Israeli civilian population centers as suicide bombers.

Targets hit were definitely not military. A bar in Tel-Aviv, the Hebrew University Cafeteria, destruction of restaurants with innocent civilian Israelis in them – these were the main targets. Nevertheless, despite what it seems to be a united front against the Jewish people by Muslims, anti-Semites and neo Nazis combined, all signs indicate that this ancient culture and it's people will survive and flourish.

CHAPTER THIRTY TWO

Now that Barak Hussein Obama was elected president of U.S.A., which many believe is a Muslim at heart (his close friendship, sympathy and association with Farakan's Nation of Islam, and other Muslim organizations, is proof enough of his inner convictions), Israel is beginning to feel the pinch. As a result, everybody, big or small, is telling Israel what to do, including dictators, murderers, fortune seekers by association with oil producing countries as well as naïve politicians.

They all seem to demand that Israel commit suicide to solve their problems. What's worse is that none of them see anything wrong with it.

The Holy Land is ancient Israel, where the twelve Hebrew tribes lived and prospered and the Bible's Old Testament came into existence. Both sides of the Jordan River belonged to original Israel. Giving the West Side of the Jordan River to the Hashamites by British politicians was bad enough, but nowadays "friends", like the British, the French and the Germans, along with United States, want to give away the rest of the land to Muslims who strive to conquer and dominate us all. Israel is now pressured to agree to the Saudi Peace Plan (in other words: a death plan in disguise) which advocates limiting Israel to the 1967 ceasefire lines, accepting big numbers of Palestinians to resettle within these borders and compensate the rest.

And what exactly would Israel get in return?

A vague declaration of promises: recognition, and security. Whether these are verbal or paper promises makes no difference: the Koran allows the Muslims to lie and cheat as long as it'll benefit their religious dictates. Denying it is avoiding the truth, and history is the best evidence.

In the past, all agreements with the Palestinians were honored by Israel but they were never honored by the Palestinians. In 1951, Israel, Egypt, Jordan and Syria agreed to cease hostilities and negotiate instead following the beating they took in the War of Liberation of 1948 from the Israeli armed forces. In 1956 the same countries attacked Israel without provocation from the South (Egypt), the North (Syria) and the West (Jordan). They were defeated and as a result they lost more land to Israel as well. Agreements to stop hostilities were made again.

For over ten years of relative peace, having time enough to replenish and reorganize their forces, friction was initiated again. Anwar Sadat, the Egyptian President, was quoted by the media as saying that real peace with Israel will come only after they'll be able to destroy at least one Israeli division. 1967 was his last attempt to achieve that goal.

Despite agreements to stop hostilities, Egypt and other Arab countries attacked again on Yom Kippur, (the Day of Atonement) the holiest day of the Jewish religion, only this time Iraq and Lebanon joined the pack – and once again they were devastated, after which Egypt and Jordan signed peace agreements following a US offer of bribes with billions of dollars. The peace agreements aren't really peace agreements: Egypt and Jordan didn't establish cultural and economic ties as promised, and when Israel was antagonized by terrorist organizations, they always justified their actions.

And now, should Israel agree to the Saudi Peace Plan and have the Arabs sign pieces of paper, trusting them to keep the peace is like entrusting the cat to guard the milk. In effect, what's the guarantee that after Israel will be made impotent, that they will honor any peace agreement?

Israel is now urged to give up old Jerusalem, relinquish control of the Western Wall, the only remnant of King Solomon's temple, accept additional Fifth Column Palestinians on top of one million who were permitted to live in the Israeli territory. They have more rights and privileges than in any Arab country, yet they claim to be Palestinians, not Israelis despite being citizens of Israel with full rights and no obligations. Moreover, they dare suggest that Israel should pay compensation to the rest of them, including their descendants. Last but best: return the Golan Heights to Syrian hands so that they may terrorize Israeli farmers from the Heights as they did for many years when they controlled it – what would the next step be? Nobody would admit that such a one sided policy would only encourage the Muslims to attack again.

Should any of the above be materialized, it'd be the first stage in the plan to destroy Israel as we know it. No one mentioned that the Muslim states forced over one million Jews to flee while their properties, valuables and businesses were taken over by these regimes. If you compare financial losses of the Jewish people forced out of their homes to the Palestinian demand of compensation for their old homes, I'm sure the Muslim States will have to compensate the Jewish refugees many times over.

Yet, no one mentioned that fact.

Not too many "friends" even want to hear about it.

However, if the above demands are enforced by Obama's U.S., the European Union, and the so-called International Community, there'll be no need to nuke Israel out of existence: Israel will be gone, anyway.

If that's not enough, and tiny Israel will be reduced to ghetto size, with a Palestinian State next door dreaming of conquest, Iran will have no trouble using their almost ready nukes against the Jewish state, and take over the oil reserves in the Middle East as well.

If that happens the future of the world will be forced praises to Allah, forced conversions by the sword, beheading opponents and enforcing the Sharia Law. Should the above plans be activated and realized, the International Community's silence will enable Radical Islamists to take over Europe by intimidation, plus exterminate anyone with a trace of Jewish blood, thus continuing where the Nazis left off.

Nevertheless, any student of history will find that the nation of Israel survived close to six thousand years, while bigger and more powerful nations vanished without a trace.

History repeats itself is true, it was so time and time again.

THE END

Made in the USA
Monee, IL
08 July 2020

56699173R00103